This book will make you dangerous

The Irreverent Guide For Men
Who Refuse to Settle

TRIPP LANIER

Professional coach and host of
THE NEW MAN

"You become dangerous, not when you're a threat to others, but when you become a threat to the excuses and bad habits that have held you back in life. Tripp's book lives up to its title; it's a practical guide for the path of self-mastery. Only then are you truly dangerous."

Phil Stutz
Co-author of The New York Times bestseller *The Tools and Coming Alive*

"This Book Will Make You Dangerous is a call to wake up, get over ourselves, and focus on what really matters."

Barry Michels
Co-author of The New York Times bestseller *The Tools and Coming Alive*

"Mindset. Strategy. Execution. Tripp is able to draw out the best in guys while also staying focused on what truly matters. *This Book Will Make You Dangerous* goes beyond chasing results. It helps us tap into meaning."

Eric Davis
Former Navy SEAL sniper instructor, author of *Raising Men*

"Tripp Lanier is a very funny guy. He's also a very wise guy. If you like to laugh deeply while bringing more playfulness and joy to your Optimizing (with a more than slightly irreverent guide), then I think you'll enjoy this book as much as I did. Tripp's a fantastic coach to help us reclaim our inner authority and live with more freedom, aliveness, love, and peace. TODAY!!"

Brian Johnson
Founder + Leader of Optimize and Philosophers Notes

"Tripp breaks the mold when it comes to how he helps people. His interviews, his coaching, his writing — it all stands out. It all leaves a lasting impact."

Daniel Priestley
Founder, Dent Global and best-selling author of *Entrepreneur Revolution*

"Feeling better long term requires outside perspectives. I've been seeking Tripp's opinion throughout the past decade of my life, for various reasons on numerous occasions. Tripp has a keen eye for next steps and confident settings. We need mental, physical and spiritual resilience through life and many people I've met along the way could benefit from his experience and observations much as I have. This book could be a life saver for a lot of people."

Dr. Eric Goodman
Founder of Foundation Training and author of *True to Form*

"Tripp has an uncanny ability to make incredibly accurate observations about human behavior and share them in a way that's candid and constructive without being a complete dick. Read this book. You'll be better off for it."

Jeff Boss
Author of *Navigating Chaos: How To Find Certainty In Uncertain Situations*

"Tripp Lanier not only stays up to date on what helps us make positive changes, he actually helps people implement those changes. *This Book Will Make You Dangerous* is an onramp into that experience."

Jamie Wheal
Executive Director, Flow Genome Project and co-author of *Stealing Fire: How Silicon Valley, the Navy SEALs, and Maverick Scientists Are Revolutionizing the Way We Live and Work*

Copyright © 2020 by Tripp Lanier
Illustrations copyright © 2020 by Tripp Lanier

All rights reserved. This book or any portion thereof
may not be reproduced or used in any manner whatsoever
without the express written permission of the publisher
except for the use of brief quotations in a book review.

Printed in the United States of America

First Printing, 2020

ISBN 978-1-60842-214-2

Lanier Creative Services, Inc.

www.TrippLanier.com

Table of Contents

What Does it Mean to Be Dangerous?. 7

INTRODUCTION 9

CHAPTER 1: Is Success Making Us Weak?. 19

CHAPTER 2: Moving from Fear to Strength. 33

CHAPTER 3: Building a Fire — Aligning Your Actions
with What Makes You Stronger 61

CHAPTER 4: Expect Resistance — Use Your Excuses
to Take Smarter Action 75

CHAPTER 5: Be Bold — Lean into Discomfort
and Develop Self-Leadership 89

CHAPTER 6: Be Playful — Minimize Risk and
Create on Your Terms 119

CHAPTER 7: Get Over Yourself — Live as if
There's Nothing to Prove and
Play for Something Bigger. 147

CONCLUSION 171

ACKNOWLEDGEMENTS 177

ABOUT TRIPP LANIER. 181

NEXT STEPS 182

What Does it Mean to Be Dangerous?

First off, let's describe what it does not mean.

In the context of this book, dangerous does not mean being disrespectful, harmful, or reckless towards our lives or others. It's not even advocating a rebellious, reactive, or "punk" attitude. The ideas in this book will not encourage you to be an impulsive, irresponsible, or hedonistic dick.

So then, what does it mean to be dangerous?

Even though there are genuinely major problems in our modern world, most of us are living with a level of comfort, safety, and self-importance that was unimaginable just a few decades ago. We've quickly adapted to these advantages, and many of us have gotten softer, more isolated, and more self-absorbed as a result. Which, as we'll explore later on, wouldn't be that big of a deal if it wasn't killing our ability to enjoy the good fortune and opportunities we already have.

So for the purposes of this book, being dangerous is about cultivating self-awareness, leadership, and the guts to steer directly into the situations that most are trying so hard to avoid. It's a willingness to occasionally rock the boat in order to live fully during our short time on this planet.

And to those that are committed to the illusion of everlasting comfort, safety, and measuring up, this way of living will seem downright dangerous.

Is This Book Only For Men?

Good question. Is this book only for men?

The short answer: it's not.

The longer answer: I've primarily taught and coached and facilitated groups of men since 2005. Working with certain types of men is what I know best. That said, the ideas and concepts and practices in this book are available to anyone and everyone who wants to take them for a test drive.

Everyone's welcome to the party, but keep in mind that the language and tone are geared towards helping the types of men I know best.

Introduction

That Time I Went to the Doctor About My Butt

When you open up a book about the big, serious topic of transforming our lives, relationships, and professions, you probably expect a quote from one of the great wisdom teachers of the past. Maybe Rumi, Joseph Campbell, or one of those stoic guys whose name looks like a little kid dropped his alphabet blocks on the floor. This is how the author sets the right tone and proves he's got some depth and should be taken seriously.

But that's not how we're going to start this book. Instead, I'm going to tell you about the time some guy stuck his hand in my bum.

Buckle up. Here we go.

One day, I go to the doctor because I have some weird pain in my butt. As I walk in the office, I see a beautiful nurse. *Wow,* I think. *She is stunning.* And then my vanity kicks in. *Oh, man. I sure hope she doesn't have to see me with my pants down. You know, I mean — not like this.*

Eventually I find myself in the privacy of that fluorescently lit tomb called an examination room, sitting on the table with that crinkly paper and the anatomy diagrams on the wall. The doc comes in. We talk about my situation, and with a bored drawl, he says, "All right. I'll be right back."

Door closes. Tension builds. Long exhale. Shaky leg.

Thirty seconds later, he walks back in with Nurse Stunning. *Shit.*

Doc says, "Okay, Mr. Lanier, please take down your pants, and let's have you bend over against the table." As I face the wall, I hear the gloves going on. I hear the bottle of lube fart out a bubble as he smears it onto his hand. *Shit.*

I'm aware that this isn't going to be an afternoon at the spa, so I appreciate that he doesn't give me the customary, "You might feel a slight discomfort" song and dance. That said, I'm still caught off guard when Dr. Bigmitt jams his way into my rear end. *Holy hell.* I involuntarily let out a low howl which sounds like a sad puppy. As sweat begins to bead on my forehead, my vanity kicks in again. I wonder if the nurse heard it.

Of course she heard it.

The doc is digging around my caboose as if he's lost his car keys. And just when I think he's finished, he decides to, in my best guesstimation, see if he can touch my tonsils. That's when I hear his frustrated voice over my strained breathing.

Dr. Bigmitt: "Umm, when was the last time you had a bowel movement?"

Me (grunting): "A few hours ago?"

Dr. Bigmitt (huffing and pissed off): "Well, there's still stool in here!"

Shit.

Me: "Doc, you chose this profession. You had to know that if you were going to play roto-rooter in people's asses for a living that you'd also encounter a poo on deck from time to time. That poo's in the right place. Your hand is not. I mean, how many years of medical school did you go through? Because I didn't go through any, and I can tell you with great confidence that you're probably gonna find a poo if you're digging around someone's butt. Jeez, man. What the hell were you expecting?"

Okay. I don't actually say any of that, but I am struck by the fact that he seemed so disappointed to find a surprise behind door number two. What *was* he expecting?

So let's start there. Let's connect the dots between this questionable way to open a book and creating the lives we truly want. Let's talk about expectations.

What if Success Isn't the Same as Strength?

I love having nice things. I love feeling comfortable and secure. And I'd be lying if I didn't admit that I also love feeling like I'm somebody special. I invite you to come clean and admit that you like some version of these things, too. Because as we're going to explore further in this book, it's natural. It's who we are. It's why we place so much importance upon being "successful" — whatever that may mean to you.

As a professional coach — someone who's spent many years working directly with people to create the lives, relationships, and businesses they truly want — I spend my days talking to extraordinary men all around the world. I'm talking about everyone from founders who have bootstrapped companies and sold them for millions, to executives who have shaped the technology we use every day, to Navy SEALs who have experienced and survived the unimaginable.

As their coach, I get to see behind the impressive displays. I get to see that many of these guys are quite confused. Even though they've got money and comfort and a sense of importance, because of their mindset, success isn't quite what they expected it to be.

That's because whether they're aware of it or not, they often have an expectation that success — on its own — would mean they would be "set." They had an expectation that success — on its own — would shield them from the pain in the ass that is life. They had an expectation that success — on its own — would bring lasting fulfillment.

For years they sacrificed and deprived themselves of so much in order to achieve so much only to find that they still felt perpetually stuck in a cycle of "same shit, different day." Even though they had jumped through hoops and accomplished what they set out to do, life was still a chronic pain in the ass. All of this left them feeling a lot like that doctor staring at his glove. *What the hell is this shit?*

This is why I throw most of the "success" how-to books I receive right into the trash. As the host of *The New Man*, a men's personal growth podcast that's been running for over a decade and has millions of downloads, I get submissions for new interviews every day. But, unfortunately, many of these well-meaning authors and "experts" are really just trying to help us get better at playing a game we can't win.

It's a game built upon this false expectation that if we just have *more* money, attention, information, productivity, technology, abs, influence, spirituality-ness — you name it — then we'll be "set for life." It's a false hope that conditions us to believe that the answer to our problems and challenges and dissatisfaction is *more* stuff that we don't really need. But very few of us understand that it's this never-ending striving for *more* that keeps us on the hamster wheel. It's this herd mentality — the comparisons to others and fear of missing out — that distracts us from what's most important. It doesn't matter if you're a corporate executive, a start-up founder, or just a guy running his own freelance gig from the kitchen table — we can create a rat race out of any given situation. It doesn't matter what tax bracket or neighborhood we live in — no one is immune.

And it's this mindset that is making us weak. Think about it. How often do we use "success" to justify doing things that *literally* make us weak?

The missed workouts. The lack of sleep. The lousy food choices. The lack of personal time. The lack of play. The withering relationships. The tolerating of assholes and ass-kissers and adversaries. The crowded, polluted living areas with astronomical costs of living. How often do we ask ourselves, "Is the stuff I'm doing to be 'successful' really making me stronger? Is this deprivation aligned with what I *truly* want?"

The reality is, we can't just blindly follow this stinky expectation that scaling or hustling or adding a zero to our net worth will create the deep satisfaction and fulfillment we truly want. And I've spent enough time meditating with so-called spiritual masters to know that we don't have to sell all of our stuff, shave our heads, and change our name to that of some yoga pose in order to experience greater fulfillment either.

Ditch the Herd Mentality and Forge Your Own Path

The good news is that in this book I'm going to share the lessons I learned from spending years down in the trenches. I'm going to share what has helped real people to break out of this rat-racer pattern to create success on their own terms. I'm going to share much of what I've learned through personal experience, from interviewing hundreds of folks who dedicate their lives to this conversation, from reading gazillions of books, and from being coached by some of the most insightful men and women who guide folks to forge their own paths.

Forging our own path. This is the foundation of being "dangerous." Not because it will necessarily put us in harm's way. In fact, as we'll learn, it helps us stay out of traps. But it does require us to create our lives in a way that most just can't comprehend because they're so committed to playing it safe — even when it exhausts them and limits them and makes them weaker as a result.

Here's what I mean...

Instead of whipping ourselves with fear, pressure, or scarcity for motivation, we're going to learn how to identify the bullshit conditioning that keeps us chasing after a magical expectation. Instead of being distracted by comparisons, pissing matches, and the fear of missing out, we're going to practice tapping into our own sense of authority for direction.

Instead of feeling stuck in a rut, we're going to develop what has us feel more expansive and free. Instead of tolerating a *Groundhog Day* existence of "same shit different day," we're going to create small experiments and identify what makes us feel alive. And instead of hoping we can find relief if we just outrun our problems, we'll cultivate the deep sense of peace that comes from knowing we can handle whatever comes our way.

We're going to expect resistance and procrastination to show up. So we'll also practice some basic ways to turn our excuses and anxiety into action. And then we'll also practice an ancient skill that most have forgotten so that we can be fast on our feet, solve problems, and bounce back after a fall.

Bottom line: We're going to ditch the unconscious expectations and patterns that make us weak. We'll learn how to align our actions with a version of success that makes us truly strong. We'll create greater alignment with what makes us stronger *today* instead of when — or if — we cross some fantasy rat-racer finish line. And as long as we don't take ourselves too seriously, it'll even be fun.

This process isn't for everyone. As I said before, all of this will seem dangerous to those who are unwilling to challenge the unconscious motivations and expectations that drive their choices.

A Couple of Things to Consider Before We Dive In

First — you may have noticed a word that popped up a lot in that list. *Practice.*

There's another reason why I'm not crazy about most of the personal and business development books out there. And that's because in their efforts to be very polished and groomed and homogenized and catchy and sellable, they fuel an expectation that growth is a linear, predictable, step-by-step process like building a Lego castle.

They often give folks the impression that lasting growth and change is really boiled down to *knowledge* — to understanding a few simple ideas. This belief leads many folks to think that devouring information through books and podcasts is the same thing as doing the work.

But it's not.

Unlike those who peddle false hope from the safety of their computer keyboard, as a coach, I'm in the trenches working with real people going through real *transformation*. *Information* is just one small part of the process. While new ideas and information are important, nothing compares to what happens when we roll up our sleeves and do smart work. Without *implementation*, information just becomes entertainment.

As you read this book, I want you to *practice* this stuff. I want you to use these ideas as a springboard to get into action. I want you to experiment, to get dirty playing on the field of your life.

So here's a suggestion — don't believe a single word you read until you test it for yourself. Please keep whatever works for you, and then ditch whatever doesn't. I'd rather you reject these ideas after experimentation instead of parroting them just because they sound good.

And second — I'm not going to pretend to be some guru, some guy on a pedestal who has all of the answers. I'm not going to lie and say that I'm somehow immune to the ups and downs of life. Any guy who tells you otherwise is full of shit. There's a reason why I still hire coaches and study and practice. It's because I'm still figuring this stuff out, too. Life is an unfolding series of challenges. I want to be clear that there's no promise of a finish line here.

Consider that I'm in this process *with* you, shoulder to shoulder. Instead of mimicking what some blowhard on a stage has to say, this book is an invitation to tap into our inner authority — that awareness of what makes us strong — and then forge our own unique paths together. It's through this process that we align our actions with what really matters and what really works.

So with that said, if our choices are driving so many of us to run the rat race, then let's start by taking a hard look at what motivates those choices. And we can do this by shining a big bright light on the romantic, magical fascination folks have with the idea of *purpose*.

Free Bonus: Video Guide

Everybody learns differently which is why I created a video guide for *This Book Will Make You Dangerous*.

And because you own the book, you can access these videos and resources for free.

You can sign up at:
TrippLanier.com/Bonus

Here's what you get:

- Videos for Each Chapter — we'll discuss the big takeaways so you can put them to use.

- PDF Files to Help You Take Action — Each chapter includes a PDF file that walks you through the exercises.

- Deeper Insights — Explore deeper insights not included in the book (as well as a few surprises).

Again, it's 100% free. Sign up now, and you'll gain instant access to the course.

You can sign up at:
TrippLanier.com/Bonus

CHAPTER 1:

Is Success Making Us Weak?

Why Your Big Life Purpose Story Is Probably BS

Most of us believe that "living our purpose" means having some remarkable story, a fancy bow to wrap around our reason for being alive. *It all makes sense now! This is why I was born! Now I have direction!* These stories typically make the purpose of our lives based on some kind of an outcome or result or process like:

> "My purpose in life is to support and empower (insert favorite group of people here)."

> "My purpose in life is to start a foundation that helps (insert favorite cause here)."

> "My purpose in life is to save the planet from (insert terrible planet-threatening thing here) and then, you know, get the original members of Van Halen to play my birthday party."

Those kinds of stories may *sound* good, and having a great story to tell the world can certainly make us *look* good, too. These "purposeful life" stories can provide us with a role to play, they give our existence a sense of meaning and direction when things feel chaotic. They can guide us to create a legacy, something to help us believe our lives were worth living long after we're gone.

But contrary to popular belief, we don't need to be aware of our life's purpose to live with a purpose. After all, even zombies have a reason — a unifying *purpose* — for stumbling around. They want tasty brains.

Whether we're aware of it or not, we're already living with a very strong sense of purpose. And to reveal this purpose, we just need to take a look at our choices. But let's be clear — this "life purpose" may not jive with the inflated, important story we like to tell about ourselves.

The Three Big Threats

Imagine you had an app on your phone that tracked every single little choice you made throughout the day. Then imagine that it went a step further and magically determined *why* you made that choice. Imagine it could figure out the *purpose* behind every choice and action.

For instance...

Why you chose to wear that shirt. Why you chose to eat that breakfast. Why you chose to take that route to work. Why you even chose to go to work. Why you chose those words in your email to the client. Why you chose to ignore that other email from the other client. Why you chose to turn down that dinner invitation. Why you chose to keep all of your stuff in the same house and continue living in your town. The list of choices — big or small — goes on and on and on.

Now, if we could slow down and evaluate each one of these choices, we would start to see the golden thread — the reason, the why, the *purpose* — that links all of our choices together. No matter what kind of fairy tale we like to tell ourselves about the purpose for our lives, this pattern will tell us the truth about what we're doing every day and why we're *really* doing it.

And for most of us, almost all of our responses to whatever happens every single freakin' day can be boiled down to answering three basic questions...

Number 1: "What do I do so that I don't feel uncomfortable?"

It's obvious that we don't want to feel too hot or too cold or hungry or physically uncomfortable in any way. But discomfort — or tension — can also be mental and emotional. For instance, effort alone is a pain in the ass. There's pressure and overwhelm that shows up when we have a deadline. We might get anxious in a social situation when the conversation's all stiff and awkward. We may tell little lies or walk on eggshells around our lover because we're afraid to get into a fight and feel hurt or angry. Even a long flight without some form of entertainment might mean hours of being bored out of our minds, trapped inside our thoughts along with the smells coming from that guy sitting in the next seat.

But let's ratchet it up another notch. What happens if we imagine we'd have to move into a house that's half the size of the one we're in now? What happens if we imagine giving up the coffee or screens or ice cream or alcohol or weed or porn that we rely on to soothe ourselves every day? Yikes.

All of this points to our deep desire to maintain whatever level of comfort we've become attached to. And if you're like most of the guys on this planet, you may tolerate a lot of crap and do stuff that ultimately makes you weak in order to stay in your comfort zone.

Oh man, I would "die" if I had to go a month without my morning coffee, a big screen TV on Sunday, or internet access.

Bottom line: let's consider that in our modern, cushy lives a threat to our sense of comfort can *feel* like a threat to our survival. We will go to great lengths to avoid discomfort physically and emotionally.

Number 2: "What do I do so that I don't miss an opportunity or put something I care about at risk?"

We all want a sense of *certainty* about what's going on and what's going to happen. We all want a sense of *stability* and the ability to *control* what's happening. And we most certainly don't want to lose something we have or miss out on something we don't yet have.

In our modern, highly sheltered lives, safety and security mean something different. Because we're no longer protecting our lives by hiding in caves or outrunning critters with big teeth, our "evolved" sense of safety has largely adapted to protecting our resources like time, energy, and money — especially money.

But as we'll discuss later, when we're unconsciously steered by our primitive wiring, we tend to drastically overestimate the dangers in our lives. Missing out on a juicy opportunity can seem like the end of the road. We often assume the worst will happen if we take a loss. We often imagine taking a risk will lead to a devastating turn of events where we end up homeless and selling hand jobs in a bus station bathroom just to get by.

So if you're like most of the guys on this planet, you may tolerate a lot of crap and do stuff that ultimately makes you weak in order to feel safe — to protect your income, resources, and opportunities.

Holy crap, I would "die" if I lost my business and burned through my savings.

Bottom line: let's consider that in our modern, cushy lives, a threat to our resources can *feel* like a threat to our survival. We will go to great lengths to avoid anything that puts our time, energy, or money at risk.

And then comes the big one...

Number 3: "What do I do so that I don't look like a loser?"

The specifics of humiliation or looking bad or strange vary from person to person. Some of the more common things guys tell me they absolutely *have to* avoid are being seen as a loser, a wuss, a nobody, a showboat, a bully, a poser, or a fraud. Many other guys are striving to make sure they're not seen as someone who's needy or desperate or mean or unfair or stupid or mediocre or arrogant or boring.

This topic of self-image gets complicated very quickly, but at the root of this desire to avoid looking like a douche-poof is our hardwired need to *belong* — to feel like we matter, to be accepted and loved. Back in the good old barefoot nomadic days when we were eating twigs and bark and smelling like Yoda's asscrack, we were dependent upon each other to stay alive. Which meant that if we did something stupid and got kicked out of the group, we would die. So nature made sure that our brains evolved accordingly, and this primitive fear of being cast out is still part of our wiring today.

Which means, again, if you're like most of the guys on this planet, you may choose to contort yourself, hide out, or play the chameleon in your relationships in order to protect your self-image. You may choose to betray who you truly are and what you deeply value, just so you can avoid the possibility that somebody might judge you or belittle you in some way.

It would "kill" me if I did something humiliating. It would "kill" me if the world singled me out and roasted me for a mistake I made. It would "kill" me if my family and friends turned their back on me.

Bottom line: let's consider that in our modern cushy lives, a threat to our self-image, status, or sense of belonging can *feel* like a threat to our survival. We will go to great lengths to avoid anything that might make us feel inferior, judged, or rejected.

So what does this all tell us?

Our Modern-Day Survival

All day, every day, we're *unconsciously* running through a cascading matrix of options in life, but regardless of the story we tell ourselves and others, the lives we have today are most likely a product of answering these three basic questions:

What do I do so that I don't feel uncomfortable?

What do I do so that I don't lose time, energy, or money?

What do I do so that I don't look bad?

In other words, when we're running on autopilot, our choices to avoid "danger" can be boiled down to protecting, pleasing, and proving.

Protecting — covering our ass, making sure we don't do anything to feel discomfort or put ourselves at risk.

Pleasing — keeping the peace and making sure we don't rock the boat with regards to the people we care about.

Proving — doing what we've got to do to consistently signal that we belong, that we're worthy, and that we matter.

This defensive decision-making process is hardwired into our system. It happens instantaneously and unconsciously, and it's at the core of our "survival" in this modern world.

But what about our big life purpose, our high ideals, and those foam-core vision boards?

Jonathan Haidt[1] is the author of several books including *The Happiness Hypothesis* and *The Righteous Mind*. He's also a moral psychologist which means that — in very technical, academic ways — he studies and writes about how and why we make choices. When I interviewed him about this gap between what we do and why we actually do it, he said, and I quote, "We're full of shit." We may like to believe that we're living rational, purposeful lives, but most of the time our unconscious fears, defenses, and desires to belong are driving most of the choices we make. Like a PR rep for some evil corporation, we're just really good at making up "logical" justifications for our fear-based choices after the fact.

Which all means that whether we know it or not, most of us are already living with a very clear, very committed *purpose* to avoid "danger" — to avoid discomfort, to avoid risks to our time/energy/money, and to avoid humiliation.

So what does all of this protecting, pleasing, and proving have to do with "success"?

When Success is Just Survival in Drag

When evolutionary biologists talk about success, they don't describe Ferraris and yachts and taking private jets out to Burning Man. They talk about our ability to adapt in order to *avoid* danger. They talk about our ability to *move away* from the critters and diseases and poisonous icky things that are trying to kill us. For eons, the standard for success meant that we avoided danger long enough to get someone pregnant and then hoped someone lived long enough to help those babies become independent out in the big bad world. (If you ask me, the females got the stinky end of the stick on that one — deep bow to all the childbearing and child-rearing superheroes.)

---

[1] He did, in fact, literally say this. Check out my interview with Jonathan Haidt on The New Man Podcast.

So success, in this case, was simple but not easy: avoid danger well enough so that we could screw and get the kids out the door. That was it. Dr. Will Vanderveer[2] is a psychiatrist who uses an integrative approach to treat PTSD and other mental health issues. He says that even though we've made so many social and technological advancements as a species, genetically our brains haven't really evolved much in the last 100,000 to 40,000 years. Our "hardware" — the systems and functions of the brain — hasn't been upgraded since we were fighting off big-ass critters that went bump in the night. Which means the brains you and I have today are still wired up to be hyper-aware of threats. We're still wired up to defend ourselves in a world that doesn't exist anymore.

So, even though we now have the ability to eat whatever we like whenever we like and find a mate by swiping the screen on our phones, I'm not convinced that our version of "success" is really that much more evolved. What I mean is, for most of us, "success" is still largely governed by the same old strategy — to get enough comfort and security and status so that we can *avoid* the stuff that feels like a threat to our modern-day survival.

Let's see. Let's play with this idea.

The Fear of Going Backwards

If what most folks consider to be "success" is the ability to acquire creature comforts, security, and significance, then it's easy to assume that the "successful" guys *must* be the strongest and bravest and most agile. It would seem that these guys would be the ones who were *most* willing to explore new scenarios, take risks, and not worry about what others thought, right?

Not so much.

---

2 Check out my interview with Dr. Will Vanderveer on The New Man Podcast.

After years of coaching high-performing men, some of the most fragile, "soft" guys I've encountered are the "successful" ones. Let me explain.

The material and status comforts vary, but the story usually goes something like this: They already have some level of success for themselves, and they're sick of playing the game they've been playing for twenty-plus years. Deep down, they want something more meaningful and fulfilling for their lives; they know they want to make a course correction, but they're also afraid to jeopardize everything they've already got.

Which totally makes sense. That said, it would seem that with their "success" — their abundance of resources and connections and experiences — they would be in a position to leverage their advantages and transition into the next phase, right?

Not so much.

Instead of focusing on all that is possible, so many of them fixate on what they may lose. Instead of getting creative, their mindset becomes very serious, very rigid. Even though they have years of valuable experiences, resources they could leverage, and a cushy net to catch them if they fall, more often than not they avoid taking any significant "risks."

That's because their primitive survival thinking has *adapted* to this elevated level of comfort. They've convinced themselves that they'd "die" if they were to take a hit or go through the dip of learning something new. Afraid to fail, to "go backwards" or look like a loser, they make excuses. They slip on those golden handcuffs. They stagnate on a flat trajectory.

That doesn't sound like success. That doesn't sound like strength. That sounds like a trap.

So is success *really* the problem?

Set for Life

Since the purpose of so many of our choices is determined by a relentless drive to protect and please and prove, it makes sense that we would want to be *done*. It makes sense that we would want to find a *finish line*. It makes sense that we would want to finally reach nirvana.

So, in an attempt to feel comfortable, safe, and accepted *once and for all*, we buy into a myth perpetuated by bedtime fairy tales, marketing companies, spiritual gurus, and religions. It's a trap that's sprung as soon as we utter the words:

Someday — once I finally have XYZ — I'll be set for life.

It sounds amazing, right? But unfortunately this misguided plan to avoid and escape the bullshit of life *for good* has a fatal flaw. And that's because every time we level up and outrun the things that go bump in the night, our primitive brains adapt. We recalibrate.

Psychologists describe this recalibration of expectations as "hedonic adaptation." It's a way of saying that no matter what we do or accomplish, our new level of comfort, safety, and status eventually becomes the new normal. And as we adapt to this new normal, we naturally just find *more* stuff to fear. We see some greener grass and believe that there's *more* to be consumed. We find new folks to compare ourselves to and believe that there's *more* to prove.

Now let's put this in perspective. Everything has a balance. The things that make us feel comfortable and safe and accepted aren't a limitation *until they are*. The things that light a fire under our ass aren't a limitation *until they are*. We absolutely *need* a certain amount of comfort, safety, and acceptance to thrive and expand. We absolutely need to have an eye on the *real* threats to our lives and loved ones. And we most certainly need to set clear boundaries against anything that seeks to harm or weaken us.

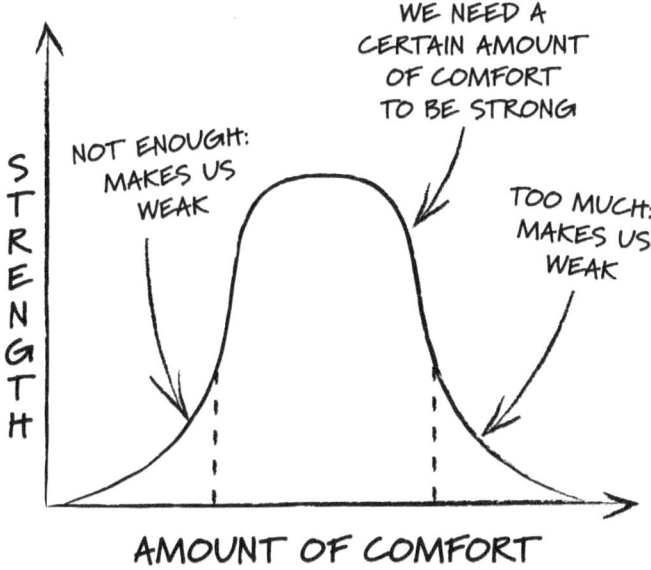

Which is good news. It means "success" isn't the problem. Nice things aren't the problem. Stability isn't the problem. And even being a hotshot isn't the problem. Trying to grow and improve our health, our income, our relationships, and our lifestyle isn't a trap. *But…*

Struggling to escape discomfort, risk, and rejection "once and for all" …
Driving ourselves like a dirty mule for that "happily ever after" finish line …
Striving to finally be "set for life" …

Yeah. That stuff is a trap.

Whether we're seeking vast amounts of cash, power, adoration, salvation, or enlightenment, it's a big cosmic joke that our efforts to *escape* suffering are usually at the core of what's *causing* our suffering. And the false hope that all of this bullshit will be handled forever once we cross that magical finish line?

That's the "hedonic treadmill." That's the rat-racer in us getting suckered into a marathon of misery because it's never enough. Our primitive brains will *always* find another threat to our sense of comfort, safety, and status.

Settling for Survival

So — what are we taking away so far?

We've learned that even though humans have evolved in miraculous ways, our primitive brains are still fixated on survival. But since we're rarely in any kind of mortal danger, we've adapted to a modern set of threats. Regardless of the story we like to tell ourselves and the world, the basic purpose driving most of our choices tends to be some combination of avoiding discomfort; avoiding risks to our time, energy, and money; and avoiding rejection. It's this deep drive to "survive," to avoid these threats, that often fuels our ambition for success. This is because, whether we're aware of it or not, most of us hope that success — in whatever form we've chosen to pursue it — will allow us to escape discomfort, risk, and humiliation once and for all.

Well, what about fulfillment? Is this reactive strategy for survival the key to a deeply rewarding life?

No.

According to Harvard professor and *Happier* author Tal Ben-Shahar, many of us aren't experiencing fulfillment because we're living in a constant cycle of deprivation and relief. When we're on the hamster wheel, our experiences tend to oscillate between feeling fearful and merely relieved. Which is another way of saying that when we're in a survival mentality, no matter how much "success" we create, our constant need to *move away* from threats means that relief is about as good as it gets.

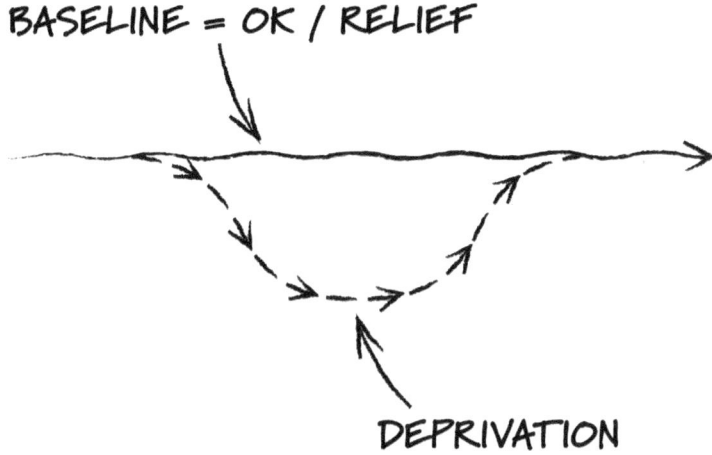

So is that it? Given all of the opportunities and possibilities in our modern lives, are we doomed to settle for relief as if we're still stuck in the dark ages?

Or can we respect our need for comfort, safety, and acceptance while also expanding what we truly want for our lives, our professions, and our loved ones?

I believe we can, and it simply begins with how we choose to see ourselves.

Prey or Hunter

Pull out your phone and search for pictures of zebras or gazelles or impalas. What do you notice about their eyes? Where are they? Yes, I'm aware that they're located on their head, but *where* on their head?

Look closely and you'll see that their eyes are on the *side* of their head. Why? Why would their eyes be on the *side* of their head? It's because they are prey animals. It's so they can more effectively scan for lions and tigers and any other big sumbitch that wants to eat them. It's so they can *avoid* them and *move away* from them. In other words, they're *genetically designed* to scan for danger so they can react quickly and run away. This design is so they can "succeed." You know, live long enough to screw and get the kids on their way.

Now do me a favor. Take a look in the mirror and tell me where your eyes are. Go ahead.

Yeah. Exactly. Our eyes are on the *front* of our head. Like a lion. Like a tiger. We are genetically designed to focus forward, to move towards what we want. Which means we are not prey.

We are fucking hunters.

Let's Keep Going

So if we want to move beyond reactivity into creativity, then we need to learn how to clarify what we truly want beyond comfort, stability, and acceptance. In the next section, we're going to practice a simple process to reveal what we ultimately want in life — and we're going to use our deepest fantasies as a starting point.

Free Bonus

Take advantage of the free video guide I've created for *This Book Will Make You Dangerous*. Each chapter includes a video and PDF to help you save time and energy.

Get it for free by visiting:
TrippLanier.com/Bonus

CHAPTER 2:

Moving from Fear to Strength

Tell Me Your Fantasies

Okay. So instead of playing not to lose, instead of fixating on our threats, we're shifting our focus towards what we want. Which means we're going to start setting goals, right?

Not so fast.

This may sound a little weird coming from a guy who makes a living helping people accomplish their goals, but, well, I'm not too crazy about goals. At least not the way most folks approach them.

Let me explain.

When I ask my coaching clients what lives in their fantasies for their "best life" or their "highest potential," they typically give me a list of things like:

- A certain amount of money in the bank
- A certain amount of business coming in
- A company sold for X amount
- More time with family and friends
- Kids in good schools and away from bozos
- Sex X many times per week
- And a big, nice house in a beautiful, safe neighborhood

Those are usually the predictable, vanilla answers. We both yawn, and I ask them if there's anything else and they say, "Naw, I'm good." And then I say, "Okay, well then tell me the stuff you'd really want if you weren't afraid to be judged, if you knew nobody would get hurt. What's the stuff you want that gets you excited, but also a little bit scared?"

Oooooh, yeah. That's when their heart rate goes up, their palms get a little sweaty. That's when they start to rattle off stuff that looks more like Tony Stark's life:

- That killer house on the coast that overlooks a private surf spot
- A custom-built education for the kids with the finest thought-leaders, teachers, and experts on the planet
- Sex whenever and wherever without guilt or shame (this one comes up a lot)
- An actual shark tank that encircles the living room and has a big pipe leading to the ocean so the sharks could come and go as they pleased (this one does *not* come up a lot)
- An eco-friendly private jet that he'd use to take his buddies on adventures to exotic locales with secret golf courses and paintball battles against special-ops mercenaries
- Hanging out around the pool with Eddie Murphy and Bill Murray
- A statue of himself in the Hall of Fame (Which hall of fame? Just pick one; I don't care)
- Oh, and what the hell — let's throw in a set of six-pack abs and spiritual enlightenment, too.

Maybe these lists look inspiring to you. Maybe you think they're a shallow, disgusting abomination in the face of almighty Oprah and your highest values. But here's the point…

Regardless of *what* gets listed, it's usually all *outcomes.*

What's an outcome? It's an observable, measurable result or event. A certain amount of money in the bank, the acquisition of a material object, an amount of time doing a certain activity, etc. And while the outcomes can be very different, they all have one thing in common:

Whether we realize it or not, these external, measurable *outcomes* all point to the internal, subjective *experiences* or *feelings* that we most want to have in our lives.

You see, a majority of the outcomes we list are unconscious *theories*. They're *guesses*. They're *assumptions*. When we imagine accomplishing an outcome we're really just imagining the experience — the *feeling* — we ultimately want to have. So when we create outcome-oriented goals, it's really our brain's way of theorizing that this accomplishment, this event, this ability to do XYZ will mean that we'll get to *feel* a certain way. Which means that behind every reasonable and outlandish fantasy that got listed above is an assumption that making this thing a reality would give us a certain feeling.

Except most of us have no clue that this is what's happening between our ears when we create outcome-oriented goals. And one thing's for certain: without a conscious awareness of the experiences we most want to have, we're likely to create a version of "success" that weakens us or feels empty. That's because we're making the mistake of committing to the outcome instead of the experience we most want to have.

Here's what I mean…

What if You Had it All and it Still Sucked?

Let's imagine we're one of those guys who grinds away for years, committed to the vision to put X million in the bank, to have the house, the car, the recognition, the sex, whatever. Let's say we actually make all of those outcomes a reality. First off, *wow*. That's impressive.

But while it may certainly *appear* to be successful, how would we *know* it was worthwhile? By comparing ourselves to others?

No. We do this by connecting the dots between those outcomes and the experiences they actually produced.

So...

What if we had all of this influence and opportunity but we still felt *trapped* because of our worries and obligations and the expectations of others?

What if we felt *drained* because we were tolerating a grind just to keep the machine running?

What if we had all of this status and recognition and significance but still felt *isolated?* What if we lost touch with our family? What if we didn't feel like we had any *true* friends?

What if we had all of these amazing things come true and we still felt *stressed and overwhelmed* because we were anxious about it all falling apart? What if we felt *bored out of our minds* because we believed everything would come crashing down if we didn't play it safe?

Because here's the deal — if we "hustled" and climbed that big mountain and "crushed" all of our goals and made our big awesome vision board a reality, and we still found ourselves *feeling* trapped, drained, isolated, bored, or stressed out, we'd have to wonder...

"What the hell is this shit? What's wrong with me? Why can't I be happy?"

As we've discussed, this happens. A lot. In addition to hedonic adaptation, it happens because we fixate on outcomes instead of the experiences we ultimately want to have.

So then — beyond comfort, safety, and status — what are we really playing for?

What Are We Really Playing For?

If we're certain that we *don't* want to create a future where we continue to feel trapped, drained, stressed, or isolated, then...

What if we ultimately want the *opposite* experiences?

Instead of trapped, we want to feel *free*.
Instead of drained, we want to feel *alive*.
Instead of isolated, we want to feel *love* and connection and belonging.
And instead of stressed or bored, we want to feel at *peace*.

Let's see. Let's test it.

Outcomes and Experiences

Try this for yourself. Grab a piece of paper, draw a line vertically down the middle of the page. In the left-hand column, write down all of the *outcomes* you want. I don't care what they are. Just make sure they're objective or measurable — meaning that they are events that can happen or not happen, dollar amounts, material objects, job titles, body fat percentages, or goals that can be accomplished. Write down things that we can observe or look at, and say, *Yup, that happened. That goal has been accomplished. That thing has been acquired. That event has taken place.*

Now, for every outcome you listed on the left, in the right-hand column write down the *experience* you imagine you'd have if that outcome became true. The experience that would make it worthwhile. Make sure it's subjective, an actual feeling. These can't be quantified. They can't be measured with some scientific device. They can only be *felt*. And this can be a little challenging, since most of us are only able to judge the difference between what feels *good* and what feels *bad*. So I'll give you a list to use as a palette, in case you need some ideas:

Relief	Whole	Fired up
Relaxed	Proud	Turned on
Stress free	Free	Admired
Comfortable	Liberated	Special
Peaceful	Open	Wanted
Content	Spacious	Appreciated
Satisfied	Alive	Loved
Aligned	Excited	Connected

Feel free to use whatever words you want, but wherever possible, drill down and see if you can get as *specific* as possible.

Now, if you do this exercise, if you write down all of the outcomes you think you really want to have in your lifetime, you can begin to connect the dots between your desired outcomes and the experiences you most want to have *right now* - not just *one day* in the future. For example...

If I had $20 million in the bank, then I'd feel relaxed and free to do or buy whatever the hell I wanted.
If I was having sex more often, I'd feel alive and excited and desired.
If I had my own company, then I'd feel really proud and satisfied.
If I had more time with the kids, I'd feel that love that was there when they used to fall asleep in my arms.

Regardless of the outcomes and the events and accomplishments you wrote down, if we look close enough we can start to see that what we ultimately want — more than to simply survive or be comfortable or accepted — is some combination of these four basic experiences: freedom, aliveness, love, and peace.[3]

Let's explore each of these a little more.

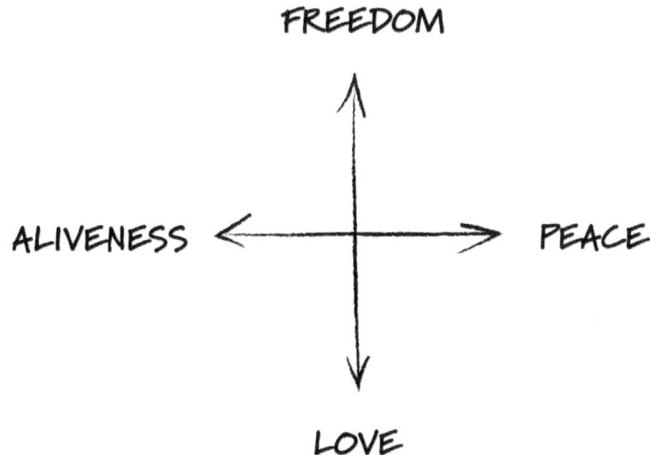

---

[3] Feel free to use the terms that work best for you. Through experience I've found that these terms offer the most flexibility and ease of understanding.

Freedom

First off, I want to be very careful that we don't create another trap here. From a prey mentality, freedom is dependent upon escaping discomfort and risk and rejection once and for all. For the people-pleaser in us, freedom is dependent upon what others are thinking and feeling and wanting. For our inner achiever, freedom is on the other side of a win or "F you money." And for the part of us that wants to be special, freedom is dependent upon securing our place in the spotlight. But as long as our freedom is dependent upon stuff we can't really control, then it's not really freedom, is it?

Most of the time, when we think of freedom we're really thinking of having lots of options and flexibility and opportunities. This form of freedom is tied to our circumstances. But if we dig a little further, we can see that freedom is actually more of a state of mind. Instead of being dependent upon wealth or status or others for our freedom, I believe we ultimately want to feel free regardless of our circumstances. *I'm free to do what I want even if it feels uncomfortable, risky, or might make me look like an idiot. I don't have to let my need to protect or please or prove stop me from doing what I want to do.*

We may express our freedom when we look at the restaurant menu and realize there's nothing on it that lights our fire. So instead of settling, we ask the waiter if the kitchen would make us our favorite entree instead. We may express our freedom when we're able to tell our sexual partner that we want to try something new and daring in the bedroom. We may express our freedom when we realize that we don't have to make so much money or "keep up with the Joneses" in order to be happy. Or we may express our freedom when we realize we can take our foot off the brake, hit the gas, and lean into our vision fully.

Beyond our desire for flexibility and options, freedom means we're able to live a life unbound from the constraints and pressure produced by our distorted fears. Freedom means we're not held hostage by our worries to look a certain way to ourselves and others. We're no longer bullied by our inner critic. And yes, we can learn to do this *without* hurting or diminishing others. Later on, we'll talk about how to own our power and authority without tearing others down in the process.

Let's keep going.

Aliveness

At first glance we may assume aliveness points to the experience of being fired up. Lit up. Passionate. Engaged. Turned on. *Hell yes!* But I want us to bring a nuanced perspective to aliveness because we're not talking about being gakked up on Bolivian booger-sugar. It's deeper. Instead of being blitzed out of our minds, it's quite the opposite. Aliveness is a deep state of presence.

Aliveness is where we feel our fire and experience a state of flow. And this doesn't happen if we're playing it safe. I believe we call this aliveness because there's a small part of us at risk of "dying" — but not necessarily in a literal way. Just listen to the language we use to describe things that have us feel alive…

When our team pulls away with the win in the last second, we may say, "We almost got killed out there." Or if we recover quickly after forgetting part of our speech in front of hundreds, we may say, "I nearly died up there."

Some of us experience aliveness when we're physically challenging ourselves — a rollercoaster, a tennis match, racing through the woods in an all-wheel-drive car sliding around blind turns. For others, aliveness shows up in moments of deep creativity, like when we design a new product and face the uncertainty of launching it into the world. Aliveness shows up when we perform, when we feel our blood racing as we plug into a guitar amp, walk up to the mic, and count off a song in front of a bar full of strangers. Aliveness shows up when we put our self-image on the line to stroll over to that cute girl in the coffee shop and introduce ourselves. And if you've ever spent a significant amount of time in meditation, you'll find that there's a deep, deep sense of aliveness that simply exists within us at any given moment if we're willing to drop the distractions and relax into the discomfort of being with ourselves.

Aliveness shows up when we've got some skin in the game — physically, emotionally, financially, or egoically. Aliveness shows up when we're willing to stretch ourselves into the areas where we may feel uncomfortable or at risk, or might look like a swamp donkey. Even though our primitive minds may try to convince us we're flirting with *literal* death, as we'll learn later on in this book, we can begin to interpret this tension as the doorway to the profound experience we deeply desire.

Bottom line, when we challenge ourselves to step into uncertainty and be bold, then we're choosing to move beyond the edge of our comfort zone. And it's at this edge where we feel most alive. Choosing to lean into this edge is where we gain energy. Even though fear may be present, we can choose to be more aware of the excitement. This can be such a powerful experience that we are often rewarded with a sense of knowing, *Yes! This is why I'm on the planet!*

Now, let's talk about…

Love

When we think of connection, it may be easy to look at all of the new technologies that allow us to communicate. But while those technologies are very effective at getting attention or finding someone to shag when we're in a new town, they often have very little to do with the deep, rewarding experience of connection — with love.

Beyond just the romantic association, love and connection point to that powerful, amazing experience of *belonging*. It's a knowing that we are truly valued and appreciated by others, and it's a fundamental need we carry from cradle to grave. Love and connection point to that experience of feeling *wanted*, knowing that we truly *matter* to someone or to those that are special to us. It's knowing that we are loved for who we are and not just the stuff that makes us look impressive. That we can reach out for help and receive it. That we can open the kimono and reveal what we're truly thinking and feeling and wanting, without fearing someone is going to use it against us later on.

And we don't just want to receive love, we ultimately want to give it as well. We want the ability to share our appreciation and care and concern for others without feeling like we're going to be judged for it.

I hope you haven't been to a lot of funerals, but it's amazing what gets said to a lifeless body lying in a coffin. So many of us — afraid to feel uncomfortable or to look "weird" — wait until that loved one is gone to express our genuine appreciation for them. But think about it — how many of our loved ones could die today without knowing just how much they mean to us or how much they impact our lives for the better?

Withholding this love robs us of the wonderful satisfaction of feeling truly connected. But the good news is that there are opportunities to do this daily if we're willing to sack up, be a little uncomfortable, and risk looking "weird." Just imagine a world where we were as quick to offer our appreciation as we were to spew our criticisms.

The truth is that love and connection can only thrive if we're willing to drop the protecting and pleasing and proving we do in order to feel safe. Love requires accessibility, it requires us to drop the masks and armor and the "I've got it all together" facade so that we can simply be who we are with each other. And if we're willing to do this, then we may discover that — more than comfort — love in all of its various forms is what we ultimately want to experience in this lifetime. Then we arrive at…

Peace

Peace points towards a state of inner well-being and equanimity. It's a calm that naturally arises when we aren't eclipsed by fear or insecurity. Fulfillment, contentment, and wholeness are all words sometimes used to point to this experience of peace. We allow peace into our lives when we aren't running away from our challenges.

Now, let's be clear — peace is different than relief or comfort or stability. As I mentioned before, we need a certain level of comfort and certainty and stability and security in our lives. Absolutely. They're essential.

So let's see if we can clear up this difference between relief and peace...

If a guy wakes up in the middle of the night with an infected tooth, he can take some pain medication to find *relief* and get back to bed. Makes sense. But unless he's a complete moron, he's eventually going to need to deal with that infection head on. No amount of pain medication — or whiskey — is going to *heal* that infected tooth. And while going to the dentist and throwing down a few bills and getting that nasty sucker pulled out may feel uncomfortable and scary, it's this healing process that will ultimately strengthen him and allow peace to return.

Let's try another one. Let's talk about comfort. In this scenario we've got a guy in his tighty-whities spread out on the couch in front of the TV. Not a problem, but like everything else in life this can get out of balance. Eventually boredom will arise and eat away at his peace of mind. *Dude. Is that smell coming from me? What the hell time is it? I gotta do something with my day.* While he may certainly *seem* comfortable from the outside, in between his ears there's a festering sense of dissatisfaction. And that's not peace.

From the perspective of our fears, we often imagine peace as a destination. It's a place we'll get to *one day* once we've figured out a way to control all of the scary, uncomfortable stuff in the world. We believe *one day* we'll finally be at peace when we have built our impenetrable castle and have enough gold and swords to keep the dragons at bay.

But peace isn't a place to get to. It's a state of mind to simply allow. And we can allow this when we recognize our strength and own our power. Instead of striving to defend and control and plan for every single possible threat, we paradoxically find a deep sense of peace when we're willing to step into discomfort, take risks, and look a little crazy from time to time.

I don't know everything that may happen, but I'll figure it out. I can adapt. I can grow. I can take chances. I can course-correct. I can learn new things. My life isn't fixed in stone.

That mindset reflects a position of strength. It's that mindset that allows peace to arise today — not at some point in the future. Avoiding our challenges — the gym, the dentist, a sweaty conversation with our wife, the tax return — may buy us a short-term sense of comfort. But it ultimately breeds anxiety. Deep down, we know that we can only kick the can down the road for so long. And like a nasty credit card bill, the longer we wait to pay that sucker off, the more it's going to hurt. All of that that kills our peace of mind.

Three-Year-Old Drunk Psychopaths

The good news is that when it comes to freedom, aliveness, love, and peace we don't have to be taught anything. It's our nature. It's our *essence*. We were born capable and ready to experience them.

Just watch a tiny kid. And I want to be real careful here because I roll my eyes at people that see toddlers as wise, enlightened beings. The fact that they sit in their own poop and believe something no longer exists just because they can't see it behind the couch has me beg to differ. If you ever spent an afternoon with a three-year-old, you'd realize that if they weighed more than a hundred pounds they'd choke you out if you turned off *Sesame Street*.

Back to my point — no one has to teach a kid how to feel free or how to feel alive or how to love or how to be at peace. If their basic needs for food and safety are in check, then their default state is usually one of complete wonder and joy. They don't have to pursue it or achieve it or strive for it or prove a damn thing. They don't even have to earn it. It's who they are. And it's who *we* are.

In fact, oftentimes it's the striving and *pursuit* of happiness that blocks us from having the experiences we most want. Why? When we fixate on what's missing — like six pack abs or hot sex with a co-worker or everlasting happiness — we can enter a dynamic that has us dismiss what we've already got. As part of the hedonic adaptation discussed earlier, we take what's already happening in our lives for granted. If we never learn how to truly appreciate who we are and what we've got *today*, then it doesn't really matter what we achieve or create tomorrow. And by doing this, we train ourselves to keep fulfillment out of reach.

So does that mean we give up creating the future that we want?

Not at all. That said, we can learn to recognize and appreciate how good we've already got it today while *also* creating what we want tomorrow. So let's take a minute to talk about appreciating what we've already got.

When I ask most of my interview guests, "What's the one thing a guy could do today that would make a big difference in his life?" Most often the answer is a gratitude practice. Period. Now, this doesn't need to be a big deal. Just set a reminder on your phone to go off several times a day, and then take a few seconds to pay attention to the seemingly minute, mundane things that are going well.

The car started. Excellent.
They got my order correct at the coffee shop. Sweet.
I woke up again this morning. Even better.

Because let's face it — when we're having a *truly* terrible day, we would gladly trade it for a mundane one. By doing this practice, we're challenged to shift our focus away from the boo-hoo baloney that keeps us stuck in the negative "not enough-ness" of life. This simple shift in our awareness will have a major impact on the way we experience our lives and find opportunities.

Bottom line: the experiences of freedom, aliveness, love, and peace I'm talking about aren't something we have to deprive or punish ourselves to earn. And like a diaper-dumping toddler who believes something no longer exists just because he can't see it, it's our fixation on what's missing that will eclipse the good fortune we already have — not just today but also the day we accomplish that goal. The good news is that we can expand our sense of peace by simply practicing gratitude for what we already have, while also creating what we want.[4]

So when it comes to freedom, aliveness, love, and peace — why don't we just call this stuff joy or fulfillment?

What's Wrong with Joy and Fulfillment?

It's easy to lump all of these experiences into one big glob and call it joy or fulfillment. Feel free to do so, but when I'm working with a guy and I ask him why he's not feeling fulfilled, often he has no idea. Fulfillment is just too vague. It's too broad.

But if I ask someone why they're not feeling free or alive or loved or at peace, then we can get specific. This helps us identify the challenge, and do something about it.

---

4 Try it right now. What are three specific things you're grateful for in this moment?

For instance...

I'm not feeling free today because I've got too much stuff on my schedule.
I'm not feeling alive today because I've been listening to attorneys ramble all week.
I'm not feeling the love today because I haven't had time with my buddies in ages. My wife and I have been distant, too.
I'm not feeling at peace today because we're trying to wrangle the next round of funding and my partner isn't pulling his weight.

When we break down joy or fulfillment into these essential components, we can ask very specific questions and get very specific answers. This specificity allows us to get proactive and take action *now*. Let's illustrate this by going through a few hypothetical coaching conversations.

What Do Your Fantasies Reveal About You?

The Exciting Empty Life

Let's say I'm working with a young buck who's all about hitting the gas in life. He's building his "brand" and he's also got his eyes on the ladies. Opportunities are everywhere, and yet — something feels *off*. So we run down the list...

"Are you feeling free?"

"Absolutely. I can pretty much do whatever I want whenever I want. I can stay out as late as I want. I can talk to any girl that I want. I've got money in the bank, which means I can splurge on travel and toys, too."

"Okay, what about aliveness? Are you feeling lit up?"

"I'd say so. My business is on the up and up. I'm interacting with cool people every day on these great projects. But..."

"But what?"

"Yeah, so that's where something feels off. Something is gnawing at me and I can't quite put my finger on it."

"Okay, then, tell me about your relationships. How's that going?"

"Well, I've got some buddies that I see from time to time. So that seems to be okay, but we're basically just going out to bars and getting loaded and hitting on girls. And I'm going out on dates with girls from time to time, but…"

"But what?"

"Man, I don't know. I mean, it's kind of fun, but it's also kind of boring having the same old 'get to know you' conversations over and over again. These girls are attractive, but it kinda feels like *Groundhog Day*. It's crazy to say this, but even if I'm having sex, I still feel bored."

"Okay, so if these kinds of interactions are no longer engaging for you, then let's play a game. If you could snap your fingers and magically change something about your life, then what would that new scenario look like?"

"Anything?"

"Yeah. Go for it. Paint me a picture."

"All right."

Pause.

"Okay, I know this sounds really shallow, but the first thing that popped into my mind was having a ton of exposure, you know? Like having people wanting to interview me and asking me for guidance on how to build their business. I'd have a ton of followers and invitations to speak at conferences, a book on the bestseller list."

"So you're saying that if these outcomes happened, you'd get *more* recognition and attention and appreciation. Is that right?"

"Yeah, but…I don't know. That comes off the top of my head, but…"

"But what?"

"I guess I'm wanting something deeper. I'm wanting to be with someone who…All right. I've got a friend and he's with this girl and they just get along so well. They do things together and just seem to really enjoy being together. I see how happy they are, and I never really thought that was possible. I always thought I'd want to put all of my energy into my work. But I'm wondering if that's changing. Maybe I'm just wanting…"

"Some depth? Genuine connection?"

"Yeah. That sounds a little corny, but yeah. And I gotta be honest, I'm really afraid to get tied down. I don't want to be trapped, you know?"

"Okay, makes sense. So would it be corny to know that someone you really cared about also really admired you and cared about you, too? Would it be corny to feel loved by someone instead of just being another date for them? And what if you could have that experience without also being trapped or 'tied down' as you said? What if this kind of relationship felt expansive for you, instead of limiting? Does that sound like something you would want to have in your life?"

"Yeah. Absolutely."

Okay, we'll cut the scene there. In this scenario, we used these four basic experiences to dial in where things felt like they were working and where they were not. From this place, we could look underneath his fantasies to see that what he truly wants — beyond *more* attention and recognition and validation — is a deep sense of connection. We could also see why he might resist going down that road — *Danger! I might get trapped! I might miss out!*

From here, we would start to align his actions with what he truly wants. Instead of continuing to exhaust himself in the shallow end of the pool, we would work on his relating skills and create some experiments where he could step outside of his comfort zone in service of what has him feel more at peace. Most importantly, we would challenge the limiting belief that having greater love and connection would somehow kill his sense of freedom and power in the world.

Bottom line: instead of waiting until he's created "enough" success or status, we can align his actions with what truly has him feel stronger today. No more waiting.

Let's do another example.

I Love — And Sometimes Hate — My Family

This is the guy who's a bit older, and he's got the wife and the kids, and for him something's feeling *off*, too.

"What's up? What do you want to talk about today?"

"Well, everything's going awesome. I mean, really awesome. Business is growing. Kids are great. Wife is great."

"Great."

"And, uh…"

"What is it?"

"I don't know. Something's off. I don't know. I keep wondering if something's wrong with me."

"Okay, let's get curious. So tell me. How are things with the family?"

"Well, like I said, they're going great. Kids are both healthy and happy. Sure, they drive me nuts sometimes, but, gosh, they're both growing up so fast. I feel like I just want to get as much time with them as I can."

"Right on. I'm glad to hear that you're enjoying them so much. And what about with your wife?"

"Uhhhhh. I mean, when we're not wrestling kids or cleaning, and we just get some time with each other, it's pretty good."

"Yeah?"

"Yeah. You know. We have some dustups here and there, but like I said it's mainly related to junk that's happening with the kids or the house or whatever. It's not about us. Does that make sense?"

"I think so. Are you guys having sex?"

"Oh boy. Uh, not really, no. I mean, I know she still loves me and really cares about me, but, no — there's not a lot of fire happening in the bedroom."

"Okay. So it sounds like, to put it broadly, you've got a lot of love and stability happening, though."

"Yeah, definitely. And when I think of it that way, I hate to sound like I'm complaining."

"I understand. We're not complaining or bitching here. We just want to get a better sense of your experience. And that said, at least right now, there's not a lot of excitement, anticipation, or aliveness happening — at least sexually. Is that right?"

"Yeah. Exactly."

"Got it. Tell me this, are you feeling flexible and free? Do you feel like you're able to shape your day and do your thing?"

Pause.

"Not really. I mean, not at all. From the time I wake up in the morning until I fall asleep at night I'm basically on duty — with the kids, with my wife, with the business. The only kind of free time I seem to get is when I take a crap and read stuff on my phone."

"Okay. And I imagine this may be part of what's gnawing at your peace of mind, right?"

"Absolutely. Like, 'When is this going to shift? When am I going to get a break?' Like, I have these fantasies sometimes where I just run away. I just wanna get a two-seater with a big engine and haul ass and do whatever the hell I want. And I feel like a jerk for saying that because my family's so awesome and, you know, so many other guys would kill to have my situation with the business and family, but I'm feeling trapped in a way, you know?"

"No problem. No need to judge it, either. We're just taking a look at what's going on, okay? And so, as you describe hauling ass through the hills in your two-seater with a big engine, I imagine that feels pretty exciting. When was the last time you felt fired up?"

Long pause.

"Uh…"

"Take your time."

"Yeah, uh, no. It's been a while. I used to race bikes, but now with the kids, you know, that's not happening anymore. But yeah, that's when I used to feel lit up. I'd look forward to the race. My heart would be pumping so hard as we waited for the starting gun. Man, I really loved that. I used to get so lit up about some of the stuff happening with the business, but now things are just cruising along, so … Excitement for me, these days, is trying to take off my son's diaper without him peeing on me."

"Okay. So we're getting that there's plenty of love and stability in your life. And that's great."

"Right."

"But when it comes to a sense of personal freedom and aliveness that's where things are not going so well. Right?"

"Yeah. Exactly."

"And all of this means that your peace of mind is going to take a hit, too. Does that sound about right?"

"Yes. That's it. Yes."

So we'll stop this exchange here. In this scenario we went from "everything's going great" to "I don't know what's wrong with me" to zeroing in on the escape fantasy that *one day* he would be allowed to experience greater freedom and aliveness. It's this imbalance and sense of powerlessness that's eroding his peace of mind.

From here, instead of blaming his situation on needing to be the "good husband," the "good father," or the "good business owner", we would find ways to allow more freedom and aliveness into his life now. In our coaching work together we would find simple ways to own what he wants and align his actions with what has him feel stronger. And we would build this strength without jeopardizing what he *also* cares about — his family and his business. No more waiting.

I'll give you one more scenario.

Hey, Babe — How About a Harem?

Here's a guy who's on the verge of getting married in a few months and he's getting cold feet. He's in a bind. He knows he really loves and cares for this woman, but he can't understand why he also wants to get the hell out of there sometimes, too.

"How are things going?"

"Oh, man. Things are great. Things are moving along fine. The wedding is in six months, and, you know…(laughter) it's a lot! It's a lot to think about."

"And what are you thinking about?"

"Well, I mean. I really love her. She's such a great gal. So many other guys would love to be with her. She's sexy and funny and…(pause) I don't know what's wrong with me. But, yeah. I mean. Ugh."

"It also sounds stressful. Marriage is a big deal. We may put on a happy face, but for many of us it seems like the end of something. Does that land for you at all?"

"Yeah. Totally."

"Okay, what does it seem like will come to an end once you get married?"

"God. I sound so shallow. I feel like such a tool. But I'm just really scared I'm going to miss out on all of these opportunities to be with other women. I was in a coffee shop this morning and this beautiful woman walked in, and I said to myself, 'You're giving this up. You're closing the door. You moron!' And it just pissed me off. I actually felt pissed at my fiancée, but she didn't do anything wrong."

"Got it. And what, specifically, do you think you're giving up?"

Pause.

"Being able to be with other women. I love women. I love that whole experience of seeing them and getting to know them and then, yeah, you know — moving into a sexual thing, you know … It's just so electrifying!"

"So it's exciting. And you're afraid you're going to be giving up excitement when you get married?"

"*Yes!* That's what it feels like. Like I'm going to be chained up and I won't have any more excitement. And don't get me wrong, like, I love being with my fiancée, but, you know, it's not the same. Does that make sense? This would kill her if she heard me talking like this. God, I feel like such a dick for saying all of this."

"I get that it's hard, and I appreciate you being straight up with yourself and with me. So, let's pivot. If you could have anything you wanted with regards to sex and women, what would that be? What's the scenario you would have, if you could rub the genie bottle and get a few wishes?"

"Anything?"

"Sure. Why not?"

Long pause.

"It sounds crazy, but I'd have a harem." (Laughing.) "I can't believe I just said that, but yeah, if I could have anything, then I'd want a harem. Full of beautiful, sexy women that would love to have sex with me and each other. Oh, man. That would be so great! (Pause.) And as I say this, I'm thinking there's no way I could bring this up with my fiancée. She would flip out. This would kill her."

"Okay, I understand. This is just the two of us talking right now. So let's look at this from another angle. If we're just talking about the *thing* you think you really want, then we're talking about a harem. And so if you had a harem, then what do you imagine your *experience* would be like? How would you know if a harem was really satisfying for you?"

"Oh man, well, it would just be so exciting. I would be able to choose who I wanted to be with. I'd always have new experiences. It wouldn't get old. Right?"

"Okay. So I think what I'm getting is that you're really wanting the flexibility or *freedom* to have the sexual experiences you want. And that you also want to feel excited and *alive*. It sounds like getting married — according to these fears and assumptions — is going to become some kind of a trap where you no longer have any juicy, exciting sexual experiences. Does that sound right?"

"Bingo. That's it. Yes. You got it."

"And so, if we were just playing hypotheticals here, if you knew that you could get married and your freedom would *expand* and your excitement and aliveness would *expand*, would that shift the way you felt about getting married? Would you feel more at peace about getting married if you knew it meant that you'd also feel more free and more alive?"

"Oh yeah. Absolutely. Big time."

"And so, what if this isn't really about having a harem? What if the harem is just a *theory* in your mind that you believe would provide you with a sense of freedom and aliveness that you truly want?"

"Hmmm. Okay. All right. I can definitely see that."

"And could it be possible that there are other ways for you to experience freedom and aliveness that don't involve a harem?"

"I mean, yeah. As we're talking about this, I'm realizing it's not really about the harem, you know? Because let's face it — having to deal with that many women could be a huge problem." (Laughter.)

"So would it be easier to talk to your fiancée about your desire for greater freedom and aliveness? Do you think she values freedom and aliveness, too? Or do you believe she *wants* to feel trapped and drained in your marriage?"

"Huh. I never thought about it like that. I mean, I'm sure she doesn't want to feel trapped or drained, either. Of course she's going to want to feel freedom and aliveness, too."

"Okay. So it sounds like you guys may ultimately be on the same page. And now it's a matter of talking about *how* you both can co-create that freedom and aliveness together. Do you think she would flip out if you wanted to talk about that with her? Do you think she would be freaked out if you were to say, 'Honey, I want to make sure that our marriage is set up so that we continue to grow and expand and enjoy our lives. I want to make sure that our marriage is something that helps us feel more free and alive as we get older together. Is that something you would want, too?' Would you be up for inviting her into that conversation and seeing where that goes?"

"Oh yeah. It still feels uncomfortable, but I would do that. That's way easier than having a harem conversation."

"Yeah. No kidding!"

We'll end that exchange here. So what are we taking away? Our guy was all jammed up because he was convinced he needed something like a harem or extramarital affairs in order to be fulfilled. He also knew it would devastate his partner, the person he loves, to hear this. All of this had him believing he was in a bind. *Damned if I do. Damned if I don't.* There's no peace of mind there.

But when we shifted our focus away from the fantasy — the specific *things* or *outcomes* he wanted — and zeroed in on the *experiences* he wanted, then he could see that he and his partner *ultimately* want the same experiences. And so, now, it was just a matter of figuring out the pathways to having those experiences.

That's when he felt like he could bring his concerns out of the dark, engage in that edgy conversation, and work towards co-creating something. He was no longer powerless. He was no longer playing the victim. In our work together, he will practice owning what he wants, being bold, and stepping into the discomfort of that conversation with his fiancée. Through this process he'll practice aligning freedom and excitement with the love and companionship he wants. No more waiting.

No More Waiting, No More Excuses, No More Fantasies

So what can we take away from all of this?

When we understand that we are ultimately playing for experiences instead of outcomes, we step into an empowered, creative way of living. It's liberating. It helps us see that all of our efforts and worries and concerns are not really about the car or the money or our kids' test scores or the harem or whatever thing or outcome or event we may have previously fixated upon. It helps us see these *things* for what they are — theories about what will allow us to feel free, alive, loved, or at peace.

When we're aware of the experiences that are out of balance, we can do something about that today. This means that instead of waiting until we've crossed some finish line or we finally earn X amount per year — we can ask ourselves:

What would allow me to experience greater freedom *today?*
What would allow me to experience greater aliveness *today?*
What would allow me to experience greater love or connection *today?*
What would allow me to experience greater peace *today?*

We can experience the enjoyment of our lives as we also create a future that we want. It doesn't have to be either/or. It can be both/and. We can take full responsibility for our state of being. We can be aware of our choices, align our actions with our deepest values, and allow those experiences into our lives *now*.

No more waiting. No more excuses. No more fantasies.

This is how we get stronger.

Let's Build a Fire

In the next section, we're going to learn how to get out of autopilot and build strength on our own terms. We're also going to confront procrastination and resistance by using our excuses to pivot into effective action.

Free Bonus

Take advantage of the free video guide I've created for *This Book Will Make You Dangerous*. Each chapter includes a video and PDF to help you save time and energy.

Get it for free by visiting:
TrippLanier.com/Bonus

CHAPTER 3:
Building a Fire — Aligning Your Actions with What Makes You Stronger

When We Don't Know What's Important, Everything Seems Important

When we don't know what's important, everything seems important. Which means that as we move forward, we want to stay laser-focused on what expands or minimizes our strength. With our primitive wiring and so much tempting drama competing for our attention, it's our responsibility to keep our awareness of freedom, aliveness, love, and peace out in front.

For this way of living, joy isn't something we only think about when we get a Christmas card at the end of the year. It's something we're aware of daily. Sounds like common sense, but as we've learned, most of the time we're focused on threats to our discomfort, resources, or self-image.

So, in order to stay off the hamster wheel, we want to identify opportunities to expand our experience of peace *right now*. Most importantly, we want to be aware of how quickly — and for how little — we sell out our peace of mind.

Here's an example…

How Much is Peace of Mind Worth to You?

One morning, a friend of mine and I were going surfing. We were standing in the parking lot at the beach putting on our wetsuits, and the day was absolutely gorgeous. The sun was coming up, the waves were beautiful, and nobody else was out. They were all at work and we were playing. Lucky us.

My friend was fumbling around with the parking meter when he realized that there would be a thirty-five cent charge to use his credit card.

"Thirty-five cents? Are you freakin' kidding me!?!" He started to piss and moan about charges for this and the unfairness of that and how it was all a racket. After a while, I said, "Hey man, I'd be happy to give you thirty-five cents." Which somehow snapped him out of his habitual bitching. He paid the meter and we were soon out in the water.

So what's the point?

In that moment there was an actual price for this guy's peace of mind. He had become so habituated to *protect* his money that he forgot what the money was for — so he could park his truck and go enjoy the freedom and aliveness and peace and camaraderie that comes from spending a morning playing in the waves. He was so unaware of the importance of his experience that he was willing to give it away for a mere *thirty-five cents*.

Now I understand that many of us are going to say it's about the principle and what's fair and all of that. And I get it, but at some point we've got to become aware of how quickly we forget what is *truly* important.

After all, let's consider *why* so many of us are exhausting ourselves to earn money in the first place. It's because we hope the striving and depriving will mean that *one day* we can enjoy a bit of relief that comes after the finish line.

But when we're habituated to struggle and strive, we simply run, run, run. We lose sight of what the effort is ultimately for. When we stop appreciating the good fortune we already have, we lose touch with the peace of mind that's available in *this* present moment. And if we don't know that our peace of mind is what's most important, then we're way more likely to give it away — or at least sell if for a mere *thirty-five cents.*

So, going forward, we want to question our choices when we're driving in traffic or reading online drama or worrying about what some twenty-four-year-old guy did on the football field. *Is this really that important? Is this really worth giving up my peace of mind?*

Commit to the Experience Instead of the Path

When we get stuck in protecting, pleasing, and proving, we can get rigid about finding "the right path" in life. But if we're clear that we're ultimately cultivating greater freedom, aliveness, love, and peace, then there are many, many ways for us to allow these experiences into our lives. Our "success" is no longer determined by what we achieved or how many years we put into an endeavor. If we're willing to experiment and be flexible with our approach, we no longer have to depend upon a vision, or plan, or path for direction.

While having a vision and a path and ideals can certainly be helpful, we don't need to let them limit us. When we understand that we're playing for the experiences we most want, we want to be willing to destroy the path or the vision or the picture in our mind if it becomes a limitation. We want to challenge our preconceived ideas of how things are *supposed* to be or how we *should* be. Why? Because it would all be for squat if following our "big plan" deprived us of experiencing freedom, aliveness, love, and peace.

This helps us see that the wheel is in our hands. Nothing is set in stone. If our path hits a roadblock, then we can recognize our choice to course-correct. If we somehow feel lost, we can always find our way again, because we know the experiences that we're ultimately cultivating.

Bottom line: instead of committing to success — whatever that might mean — let's recognize the opportunity to commit to what strengthens us. Let's commit to what empowers us to experience greater freedom, aliveness, love, and peace.

I'll tell you a little story about one of the ways I learned to implement this method of creating in my own life.

Struggling to Find the Perfect Plan

Years ago, after I sold my first company and house, I had a few bucks in the bank. I wanted to transition professionally and do something more meaningful and impactful, but I was scared to commit to any one single path. No matter what options I considered, my inner perfectionist also saw the fatal flaw, the reason why it wouldn't work. The money I had in the bank created a cocoon that allowed me to dick around and spin my wheels for years (!) — years I would never get back.

One of the reasons I was stuck is because I believed I needed to predict the future. I believed I needed to find the perfect plan that wouldn't fail. I believed I had to figure out how everything was going to directly pay off financially. I believed I needed to have it all figured out before I got started. I was doing everything I could to minimize risk, and I was scared to create a future where I would be trapped on another hamster wheel.

This mindset had crippled me. I was rigid. I was fragile. I was playing not to lose instead of focusing on possibilities. And I was embarrassed. When I talked to others I prayed that they wouldn't ask me what I was doing with my life. I was scared to tell the truth — that I was stuck and lost. On top of that was an inner critic that beat me night and day for being such a candy-ass while others were dealing with much bigger challenges. Things got so bad that I even talked to psychics and astrologers and any other weirdo I thought would give me the "key" to my future.

After a couple of years (!) of complaining and bitching and shooting down ideas, I finally reached a powerful, yet obvious realization: There was no perfect plan. No perfect path existed. No matter what there was going to be uncertainty. There were going to be risks. Mistakes were going to be made. I was going to be uncomfortable. I was going to look stupid from time to time. I was going to have to put in the work and discipline no matter what. And all of this meant I wasn't flawed. I was just afraid.

Even though I had tried so hard to avoid a trap, I had ended up creating one for myself anyway. And the more logical and rational I tried to be about it, the more trapped and drained and stressed out I felt.

You see, I had forgotten that I had already been through so much and come out the other side stronger. I had forgotten that I was able to learn. I had forgotten that I was resilient. I had let my fear convince me that being uncomfortable or losing a few bucks or making a few mistakes would mean the end of me. I had let my fear convince me that discomfort, risk, or looking stupid might be a threat to my *survival*. It sounds crazy to say all of this out loud, but allowing myself to get hijacked by my fear was far more dangerous than any path I may have chosen.

I was sick of feeling stuck. I was sick of feeling contracted. So without the "need" to have comfort and complete safety, I flipped strategies. Instead of trying to predict the "right" path and all of the uncertainties of the future, I shifted my focus to…

What will strengthen me now?
What fires me up now?
What feels expansive now?
What am I curious about now?
What do I want to learn now?

And then I took action. *Let's see.*

In the most essential way, I let go of needing to see how all of the dots were going to connect in the future, and instead I made a commitment to what had me feel more strong and expansive in the present. Instead of waiting to be inspired, I got disciplined. If I wanted to learn a certain skill, I put in the time and energy to learn that skill. I learned to expect that any learning process has a dip — call it "the suck," if you want. I didn't allow myself to quit just because things got uncomfortable, and this is where having coaches and others in my corner helped immensely.

I shifted my entire orientation to creating my life and business. I was no longer trying to find a crystal ball that would predict my future. I was no longer seeking a finish line. I was now learning to build a fire, and a fire simply needs a spark to get started. For me, that spark could be my curiosity. A hunch. If I slowed down and really paid attention to my experience, I could begin to notice where I got even just the least bit excited about something. And so I would feed that spark a little air and a little fuel. I would invest time and energy and even money into learning that thing that felt a little exciting or interesting.

Little by little, through experimentation, I learned to pay attention to my experience and see what actually had me feel more free, alive, connected, and at peace. And little by little, through consistent action, I learned what strengthened that fire and what weakened that fire.

The business I have now, my family, where we choose to live, how we choose to live — this has all been the product of experimentation. This way of living has all been the product of expanding what has us feel stronger. If we go back to this fantasy that we can predict the future and forecast the "right path" for ourselves, there's no way I could have possibly predicted what would have strengthened me way back then. This can only be learned through *experience.* When I look back in the rearview mirror of my life, I can see how all of the dots connect. It all makes sense now.

So as we go forward in this book, we're going to go much deeper into this process so that you can use it to build your own fire, to become stronger. Let's take some time to start with the basics.

What Makes You Stronger?

Give Your Brain and Body What They Need

Most often, if we're feeling drained or frustrated or overwhelmed, we believe the stories our minds tell us for why we're feeling that way. And while some of our moods may certainly be related to what's happening and what we're thinking, very often how we're feeling is a direct result of how we're treating our body.

Think about it — *all* of our experiences are governed by our physiology and our brain chemistry. Which means if we're stuck in cycles of high stress, lousy sleep, poor nutrition, and no fun time with friends, how can we possibly expect our bodies and brains to magically function well? If we're exhausted from the roller coaster that comes from sugar and caffeine and no exercise — it doesn't matter what we do — our thinking and mood and brain functioning are going to suffer.

Lousy habits produce lousy moods. Lousy moods produce lousy choices. Lousy choices perpetuate a lousy life.

Most of us are waiting until the "right time" — after a deadline or when things get "easier" — to start doing what makes us stronger. This is ass-backwards. The "right time" to do the stuff that strengthens us is when we're challenged. When we're drained or stressed is exactly when we've got to lean into it.

Which is easier said than done, I know. The good news is that a little bit every day goes a very long way. And — contrary to what our rat-racer, finish-line-obsessed mentality wants us to believe — good food, good rest, good movement, and good times with friends is the quickest way to make a dramatic shift in our life experience.

I highly recommend doing some research on how certain foods impact your mood. Sadly, so much of what seems "normal" in our Standard American Diet works directly against our brains' ability to function well, and we feel like poop as a result. I found Julia Ross's book *The Mood Cure* to be really helpful. With a few easy corrections to my way of eating, I've learned how to be much stronger mentally and emotionally. And all of this requires minimal effort to dramatically shift the way we perceive our lives and opportunities.

Let's talk about our brains a bit more.

Meditation is Strength Training for the Brain

Here's a question: if we're driving blind, if we're unaware of what we're doing or why, then how can we expect ourselves to make smart, strong choices? Without self-awareness, we depend on our primitive thinking to function. Which means we stay stuck in a prey mentality. We stay stuck on the hamster wheel.

So how can we expand our self-awareness? Meditation.

Consistent meditation is strength training for the brain. It trains us to be patient. It trains us to witness how we operate. It trains us to watch the "movie" in our minds without getting sucked into it. It trains us to slow down our primitive reactions and choose a more mature, empowered response.

Research has shown that after just eight weeks of consistent mindfulness meditation, the amygdala — the part of our brain known as the "fear center" — noticeably shrinks. And the prefrontal cortex — the part of our brain that deals with decision-making and awareness and concentration — becomes thicker.[5]

---

[5] Ireland, Tom. "What Does Mindfulness Meditation Do To Your Brain?" Scientific American, June 12, 2014.

The great news about meditation is that it's free. It's safe for the planet. And it's cheaper than taking meds. You don't need to burn incense or listen to some new age music that sounds like someone's taking a piss while a frying pan goes rolling down the hill. You can use one of those meditation apps if you want or you can simply sit still and observe your breath for five minutes a day. There's no need to make this complex. Just find a practice and do it — daily. I've been meditating consistently since my late twenties, and I can't recommend this enough. Just do it.

Creating Alignment with Strength

When we talked about purpose earlier, we considered that most of our choices are driven by our unconscious commitment to avoid discomfort, risk, and looking like a dweeb. Which means that if we want to get out of this primitive autopilot, then we want to become aware of our choices and see if they align with what makes us stronger.

Let's imagine we have a special gauge on our dashboard. As we go through our day and we make all of our choices, at any given time, we can look down at this gauge and it'll show us if we're getting stronger or weaker as a result.

For example, if we spend an hour swiping through our phone comparing our lives to a fake, photoshopped version of reality, we can check this gauge. *Is this making me stronger?*

What happens if we eat crappy food and stay up too late? *Is this making me stronger?*

Beating ourselves up to look different? Gossiping about others? Getting outraged by the news? Let's check the gauge. *Is this making me stronger?*

Not so much? Okay, good to know. We don't need to beat ourselves up about it. This is simply an opportunity to find what does build our fire. And we may be surprised by what we discover.

Depends is More Than Just a Diaper

Depends is more than just a diaper that grown folks use to poop in. What strengthens us as individuals depends on who we are as individuals — not what some blowhard on a podcast or in a book tells you will strengthen you (cough, cough). We're much better off if we're willing to drop any preconceived notions about what *should* make us stronger. Let's be willing to be surprised by what actually strengthens us. *Let's see.*

Years ago, I was coaching this guy who was in the entertainment industry out in Hollywood. From the outside, it looked like his life was really impressive. The work he did allowed him to be on a first-name basis with various artists and celebrities, and he got invited to some really exclusive experiences. Sounds like he should be stoked, right?

Well, he wasn't. In fact, he was burned out. He was rarely content. He lived with a nasty inner critic that was constantly pointing out where he wasn't enough — not making enough money, not being recognized enough, etc., etc.

He'd gotten so wrapped up in the image of what *should* make him happy and fulfilled that he really had no idea what actually did. So when we met for our coaching sessions, our first big focus was simply to help him come back to what strengthens him. That's when I gave him some homework.

I said, "Okay, let's make an agreement. This week, I want you to simply track where you feel stronger or more alive or more free or more at peace. Throughout the day, jot down some of the activities you did that were rewarding and memorable. You already do a great job of highlighting all of the things that don't seem to be going so great, so let's build an awareness of what *does* go well. Agreed?"

"Agreed," he said.

So he showed up on the next call a week later, and we started reviewing his week. I asked him, "What are some highlights? Did you find something that had you feel stronger?"

He said, "I gotta tell you. This one is kind of weird, but, uh...I went to the big hardware store to get something and while I was walking down the aisle an elderly lady stopped me and asked for my help. She asked me if I could help her find a light bulb. (Laughs.) And I don't know if she thought I worked there or what, but I just went along with it, and together she and I went over to the light bulb section and we found the bulb she was looking for. We were chatting the whole time, and she was super nice, and man, it was just really cool. And I can't explain it. It made my day. It made my *week*."

This is good data.

Let's zoom out. Here's a guy that is running a script in his head — he's got this vision, a path, an expectation that says he'll *only* find fulfillment by being more significant and super wealthy and all of that stuff. But in reality, striving to live up to this expectation keeps him on the hamster wheel. It's weakening him.

When we begin to gather data in an effort to figure out what *truly* strengthens him, we begin to see — surprise, surprise, surprise — that he was more energized and fulfilled when he was helping others, when he wasn't worrying about being somebody, when he wasn't striving to prove anything. And as we looked around, we could see that the opportunities for these experiences were much simpler and closer than imagined. If he wanted to build an empire of fame and success he could, but with this kind of data he began to see that he didn't *need* to. He could simply find more ways to experience meaning by being of service to others.

So with this information, we can expand on this idea and test it further. We can find other activities in order to see what actually strengthens him. Shifting into a mindset of strength changes everything. A stronger experience of ourselves shifts how we experience the world. As we pull our head out of our ass, we'll start to see doorways where there were once only walls.

Everything is an Experiment

Throughout this book, I've been banging the drum about how our experiences of freedom, aliveness, love, and peace are the focus. About how no matter what, goals and outcomes and accomplishments are all theories or strategies to empower us to live from this place. And I admit, to those high achievers out there who eat goals for breakfast, it may have sounded like I've been taking a piss on the whole notion of getting things done.

Quite the contrary. When we understand that these experiences are the focus, it helps us to align our actions in the service of these experiences. In other words, if these experiences are the *purpose* for what we do, then throughout our lives we'll have various *missions* — projects or goals or experiments — that empower us to have those experiences.

This means that throughout our lives, the *purpose* of what we want — to experience freedom, aliveness, love, and peace — will stay constant. But the missions — the pathways and practices that empower these experiences — will change. Missions change, but the purpose of our missions does not.

This stance will challenge us to drop the idea that there's a finish line. After all, when we're feeling trapped, drained, isolated, or stressed out, of course we would want to be *done*. But when we're expanding what we love, then we naturally want to keep going.

From this creative perspective, everything is an experiment — how we treat our bodies, how we earn our money, how we show up in relationships, where we live, *everything*. If we're willing to deal with some discomfort, risk, and the possibility of looking a bit eccentric, then we always have the choice to experiment and see what would be more expansive and empowering.

Missions Make Things Clear

When we clarify a mission, we give ourselves a clear objective. We're creating an experiment to see if this — whatever it may be — makes us stronger. In the process, we'll be challenged to be specific and disciplined.

I'm going to learn how to play this Rush song on the guitar.
I'm going to challenge my social fears by talking to three strangers every day.
I'm going to get a loan for my business.
I'm going to learn how to make $10,000 a month.
I'm going to sell my company for no less than $7 million.
I'm going to hire someone to help me start a foundation.

When we clarify a mission — no matter how small — we are now in a position to ask questions like, *What action will I take today? Who's already done this? Who can help me?* There's no need to dick around. We can simply pivot directly into action, and all along the way we're checking in. *Is this making me stronger? Let's see.* All along the way, we're saying *yes* to what strengthens us and saying *no* to what weakens us.

The good news is that we can always throttle back to what makes us feel comfortable and safe. So start small. Stretch yourself a little bit at a time. Add a little fuel. Add a little air. Build that fire.

As we do this, we can expect a bit of resistance to show up along the way. But what if we could use it to make us stronger?

Free Bonus

Take advantage of the free video guide I've created for *This Book Will Make You Dangerous*. Each chapter includes a video and PDF to help you save time and energy.

Get it for free by visiting:
TrippLanier.com/Bonus

CHAPTER 4:
Expect Resistance — Use Your Excuses to Take Smarter Action

There Are No Commitment-Phobes

Expanding our sense of freedom, aliveness, love, and peace means we're going to be moving beyond what seems comfortable or safe. It means we're going to invite *small* amounts of "danger" in the form of discomfort, risk, or failure. And you can bet your butt that there's going to be some resistance.[6]

Every so often, someone will interview me for their podcast so we can discuss why men do this and men do that in relationships. I can't pretend to speak for all men, but inevitably, I get asked some question like, "Why won't a man commit?"

And my response is usually, "It's because he's already committed."

He's committed to his sense of comfort. He's committed to his sense of safety. He's committed to his need to look good, to be accepted in his community. And if he thinks "committing" to a certain relationship may threaten these things, well, then he's going to resist. This is true for all of us. And it's true for basically anything in our lives — not just relationships.

---

[6] Check out my interviews with Steven Pressfield (author, *The War of Art*) and Phil Stutz and Barry Michels (co-authors, *The Tools* and *Coming Alive*) for their unique perspectives on resistance.

Whether we're conscious of this commitment or not, it's there — all the time. And if we can't seem to understand why we're stuck, why we're having a hard time committing to a new behavior, a new way of eating, an exercise program, or a relationship, then I'm going to put my money on the idea that in some way we believe that new thing — no matter how *obviously* good it may be for us — is somehow a threat to our sense of comfort, safety, or self-image. This means our fears will defend living in a way that keeps us feeling trapped, drained, isolated, overwhelmed, or bored out of our minds.

I have to do this draining work or else my entire life will fall apart.
I'm trapped in this lousy relationship because I don't want to be the bad guy and leave.
I'm forced to take on all of these overwhelming responsibilities or else I'll look like a failure if I go backwards.

From this perspective, we can see that there are no commitment-phobes because we are *already* committed to our survival, our "success," so to speak. Harvard faculty member Dr. Lisa Laskow Lahey and psychologist Dr. Robert Kegan call this our "competing commitment," and we would be foolish to expect to make any significant change in our lives without addressing these underlying commitments first.

Why? Because when we don't own our competing commitments, they end up sabotaging us. Like that sumbitch-nasty-one-eyed-periscope-snorkel-creature in the trash compactor from the movie *Star Wars*, it lurks underneath the surface, and then *THWOOOP!* grabs our ankle and pulls us back under when we least expect it.

If we're going to lie on our deathbed with any regrets, our regrets will have resistance to thank. So let's stay aware of our commitment to comfort and safety and acceptance. Let's expect resistance to try and convince us that a tiny speed bump is really a wall.

The first step is to learn how to identify resistance, and to do that, we can just take a look at our excuses.

Wait. This Doesn't Feel Good.

One common way to tell if we've been hijacked by resistance is if we hear ourselves say something like, *Whoa. Wait a second. This is uncomfortable. Something must be wrong. I better wait until this discomfort goes away. I better figure out why I'm uncomfortable.*

This one goes out to all of us who suffer from analysis-paralysis. It points to a belief that discomfort is somehow *unnatural*. Well, consider this scenario — we're at the gym working out. But after a few reps, we start to experience this weird burning sensation in our muscles. *What the hell is going on? This can't be right!* What if we were convinced that this discomfort meant that something was wrong?

Those that are committed to being stronger and more mobile understand that this tension is merely the physical sensation of their muscles growing and stretching. It's part of the process. They expect the discomfort. They know it doesn't mean something is wrong, even though it may be intense at times.

But what happens when we begin to feel that emotional intensity? What about that voice that says, *We better stop. This feels uncomfortable.*

It's resistance. Resistance just means we're moving outside our comfort zone. It's a universal, natural response to experience this discomfort. It's also a universal, natural response for us to try to find really compelling, convincing reasons not to do the things we want to do, because we don't want to feel that discomfort.

Resistance is committed to keeping us within our comfort zone — even if we're not happy there. And it'll do whatever it can to grab that wheel and steer us into a ditch. So instead of getting stuck in analysis paralysis, we want to remember that discomfort doesn't mean that anything is necessarily wrong.

Be curious about it? Sure. Let it control our lives or wait until it gives us permission to move forward? Not unless we want to be miserable.

We can learn to find our sweet spot with this discomfort. We don't have to be overwhelmed or crippled with stress because we've taken on too much. And we certainly don't have to stay stuck because we're avoiding it either. We don't even have to analyze or try to figure out why we have resistance. Instead, we can simply ask ourselves, *What's the very next simple step I could take?* Then go do it — let's see if it makes us stronger.

Moving on to the next excuse.

If I Make a Big Change, Everything Will Fall Apart

Let's explore another very common scenario I encounter when I'm coaching. I talk to so many clients that have big dreams and even bigger excuses. They paint a wonderful picture for themselves, and then hit a wall because they believe they'll have to do something reckless or dramatic that would endanger their family or lifestyle. It's usually some story about having to quit their job, or get a divorce, or raise vast amounts of cash before they could even get started creating the thing they want to build.

With the stakes so seemingly high, we can grind to a halt because of the "fear of failure" or even the "fear of success." Regardless, it's some belief that making this change means some huge, terrible thing will happen.

But what if these doomsday scenarios are really just another scary, made-up monster under our bed? Most of the time this kind of thing is just resistance. And convincing ourselves that the next step is reckless or dangerous is a highly effective way to rationalize staying in our comfort zone for *years*.

But when I walk through these nightmares with clients, most of the time we come to realize they're just fantasies. In reality, the next step isn't drastic. It's usually quite small, benign, and mundane. Our ego may want to believe that we're the hero who has to slay some big dragon, but what's more true is that we're just a person facing an uncomfortable conversation, phone call, or task. There is no dragon.

Here's an example.

I once worked with a guy who told me he had this huge, burning desire to start his own real estate investment company, but, by gosh, he just couldn't figure out why he wasn't moving forward.

I asked him, "What do you think needs to happen *before* you can move forward?"

He said, "Well, I would need to quit my job. And before I can do that I have to have X amount in the bank so my family is okay. And I'm just not saving it quickly enough. It's going to take years, at this rate."

I said, "Okay. Well, tell me this. What's the first thing you would do after you had all of the money saved up, knew your family was safe, and quit your job?"

He thought about it for a little while, and then said, "Well, I'd reach out to some mentors and start figuring out how to create this investment deal. I'd research what would make it work for them, that kinda thing."

"And do you really need to quit your job in order to do that?"

(Cue Jeopardy theme.)

"Huh. I guess not."

If resistance has us believing that we need to quit our job, or sell our business, or have a ton of money in the bank *before* we can do the thing we really want to do — then let's first imagine we've already done those things. Let's put ourselves in that situation mentally. Now if this were true, what would be the very next practical step we'd take?

What we're likely to see is that this step is not dependent upon our professional or financial or relational situation. We can see that this step is within reach *today*. And while it may be a little scary, it's something we can do right now.

Let's keep exploring the excuses that resistance feeds us.

I'm Just Not Ready. I Need to Be Confident. I Need to Be Inspired.

Another way to tell that resistance has infected us is when we hear ourselves say things like, *I'm just not ready to do this thing. I'm not inspired. I have to be more confident, passionate, or experienced.*

Here we are, moving forward towards the thing we want. And then — SNAP! — in comes the thought that says, *Wait a minute. I'm missing something. I can't move forward. I need to have a burning desire or more passion or more confidence or experience in order to get this done.*

In other words, when this tension naturally shows up, resistance has us believe it's a sign to pull over and wait until we've somehow magically accumulated the fire, confidence, or experience to push through the discomfort.

Unfortunately, this mentality has it backwards. What's true is that we build excitement, confidence, momentum, and experience by taking action — by learning lessons along the way. These attributes are a *product* of engaging our challenges. Waiting around for them to show up is a trap.

One day, I was on a coaching call with one of the members of my group program. He was feeling trapped in his current work situation and wanted to start his own business. Time was passing, nothing was getting done, and he claimed he was stuck because he wasn't fired up. He even said, "I'm just not passionate. I'm missing that burning desire, you know?"

So I asked him, "What would you do if you already had that burning desire?" He took a moment, and after a while, he drew up a very clear set of actions that included stuff like filing the paperwork to form his own company and making some contacts to line up funding. And so I said, "Great. You can do that this week, right? You don't need to be passionate or fired up to do that stuff. You can simply go do it. When will you contact me and confirm that you've completed these tasks?"

If we're thinking we need to be confident or passionate before we get going, let's ask ourselves, "What action would I take if I believed I was ready?" Most often, we'll see that performing this action doesn't require any inspiration on our part. We can do this thing whether we're in the mood or not. And by doing it, we'll feel our spirits lift. By doing what matters we'll feed that little spark some fuel and some air. We'll build that fire. We'll get stronger.

Here's another way to turn resistance into action.

I Don't Have the Money or Time or Energy

I'm often amazed by how much time someone may spend justifying why they *can't* do something. In an effort to convince themselves that their challenge just can't be tackled, they may spend hours, weeks, months, or even years defending and explaining why the thing they want to create just can't be done.

I just can't right now. I've got the thing coming up and then Mercury is in retrograde and then before you know it the Olympics will be happening again...

That's resistance. Resistance loves to defend and explain and justify.

But when someone really wants it — wants it enough to step out of their comfort zone — then the conversation changes. Instead of defending and explaining and justifying, they're now asking questions. *Okay, given that I've only got X amount of time, and I've got these commitments, how can I get this done? Given that I only have X amount of money right now, how can I get this done? Who can I talk to who has already solved this problem? Who can I talk to that may be able to help me get this done more easily?*

Let's keep an eye on the defending and justifying and explaining. It's a sign that resistance has got us by the plums. Instead, let's embrace our limitations and get curious instead. *Given that this is my situation, what's possible? Given that I only have this much time or money, who can help?*

But what if you don't know what to do?

I Don't Know What To Do

One of the biggest excuses I hear most often is "I don't know what to do." And what I've found to be more true is the statement, "I don't know what to do that isn't scary or risky or isn't going to make me look stupid." When we ask ourselves to come up with options that *would be* risky, uncomfortable, or possibly lead to embarrassment, then suddenly we have lots of clarity about what could be done. This helps us see that protecting, pleasing, and proving is holding us back.

One of the sneakier ways resistance does its dirty work is when it convinces us that "researching" and "gathering information" is the same as doing the work. Here's an example…

It's embarrassing to admit, but I spent two years *reading* about meditation before I actually started my daily practice with a ten-day silent meditation retreat. Which period do you think had a more profound impact on my life — the *two years* of gathering information or the *ten days* of practicing? I'll let you take a guess.

We're kidding ourselves when we think that "information-gathering" — listening to podcasts and reading books and streaming through course after course — is somehow the same as getting in the trenches and doing the work. It's not. It's tourism. Looking at maps is not the same as cutting a path through the territory. Information is just entertainment if we don't apply it to our lives.

This all points to a misunderstanding we may have about creating clarity and certainty. We don't find clarity and certainty *out there* or under some magical rock. We find it by rolling up our sleeves and getting into the process right in front of us.

Think about it — everything we use and buy and consume is the product of some sort of creative, evolving, trial-and-error process. Everything we use and buy is part of an ongoing experiment. Every iteration is an improvement over the last one. The creative people behind these products and services are able to make better and better offerings because they're already engaged in the process. This means they're able to learn from their experiences. They can't predict the future any better than the rest of us, so they solve problems by putting stuff out there and seeing what works and what does not. Even those creative teams with hundreds of millions of dollars at their disposal sometimes get a winner, and sometimes they get a pig. But if they can't predict "the best way" without trial and error, then who the hell are we to think we can?

Bottom line: let's keep resistance in check by engaging our missions. We can gain a lot of knowledge and information from books and media, but we can only gain wisdom from experience. Wisdom — learning what truly matters and what truly works *for us as individuals* — comes from trial and error. We can certainly benefit from memorizing and regurgitating the valuable knowledge that others have shared. But ultimately, wisdom lives in our bones, because of our experiences. It's these experiences that empower us to lead our lives on our terms.

Now let's talk about why kids suck.

Success Looks Like Failure in the Middle

Maybe it's our desire for completion, or maybe it's a belief that our growth is fixed, but most adults think they're done with the whole learning process after they finish school. As if they're a cake that just got out of the oven, there's a weird belief that after those early years of schooling or training, they're just *done*.

So when we're tired of the trajectory we're on and we want to make a change, often we find that in order to create that change we need to learn some new skills — could be business skills, technical skills, relating skills, whatever. But, unfortunately, this can be a deal breaker for us if our self-image won't tolerate the fact that we're going to be beginners again.

Because let's face it: Success looks like failure in the middle. Learning is where we screw up. It's where we fail. Look at kids trying to walk or ride a bike or swim. Listen to a kid trying to learn a musical instrument. They suck. Bad. Unfortunately, sucking and failing over and over again is part of the learning process, no matter what we're learning.

But if we're committed to protecting and pleasing and proving, then looking like a failure is a big no-no. If we're committed to whatever glorious story we want to tell about ourselves — *I've got my shit together, I'm in control, I'm the smartest guy in the room* — then anything that challenges our self-image is not an option.

So we settle for the excuses.

I need to save money for this other thing.
I can't justify spending time away from my family.
It's just not the right time. I've got a big thing happening at work.

But it is far more likely that we don't want to go through the challenging part of the process where we *look* like a noob again.

So here's another opportunity to remember what we're playing for, instead of fixating on what we're trying to protect. It's an opportunity to embrace the messiness of the creative process and get over ourselves. When we understand what the process is like, we can make a choice. *Am I going to play defense my entire life so that I can protect my comfort and self-image? Or am I going to go through some discomfort so that I can continue to grow and expand in service of greater joy and fulfillment?*

In a bit, we're going to explore this notion of getting over ourselves much further. But for now, let's go for a swim.

Learning and Doing Are Two Very Different Experiences

I had great parents, but let's just say parenting was quite different back in the 70's when we played with lawn darts and drove around without seat belts. One day, when I was about four years old, I remember being told I was going to go play at a pool near my grandparents' house. I'd never been in this particular pool, but I loved being in the water even though I couldn't swim. I just hated putting my head under the surface, and I damn sure wasn't going to go in the deep end.

So we're walking into the pool area and I see a woman there and a couple of other kids. No other parents. *Hmmmm.* My dad talked to the woman for a bit and then said he'd be back after a while. *Wait. What?* I remember locking eyes with him as he turned the corner. *Uh oh. Something's not right.*

It wasn't long before I realized that this was a covert black ops swimming lesson, which meant it wasn't long before that woman picked me up and threw me into the deep end of the pool. I remember screaming. I remember thinking I was going to drown.

And I also remember that I learned how to swim.

Teaching tactics aside, what's the point here? So many of us bail on the creative process because we think that the process of *learning* something is the same thing as *doing* something. And if we don't like the discomfort that shows up in the learning process, then we automatically assume that we're going to hate doing this thing when we're competent. But what if that's not true?

Learning to swim sucks compared to being able to swim.
Learning to ride a bike sucks compared to being able to ride a bike.
Learning to play guitar sucks compared to being able to play guitar.
Learning how to build a business sucks compared to being able to run one.
Learning how to market and sell your offering sucks compared to being able to do it well.

If my client says they want to throw in the towel, I encourage them to consider where they are in the learning process. Have they developed some level of competency in that particular skill yet? Or are they still in the suck of learning?

I remind them that, yes, our subjective experience is very valuable, but we also need to recognize where we are in the process. We can't expect to feel more free or alive or at peace if we're going through the suck. Going through the suck of learning something new doesn't mean it's bad or wrong. It's simply part of the process. And it's much easier to manage if we expect it.

Now, it's time for a little magic.

It's Time for a Montage

If you grew up in the 80's you saw something truly magical in almost every action movie or TV show.

It was the montage.

Let's say B.A. Baracus and the rest of the A-Team had to whoop somebody's ass. First, they needed to build a van that could launch missiles and jump a lake using lawnmower parts and an old golf cart they just happened to find in some guy's shed.

While some cheesy 80's synth-rock music played, we watched them weld things, try them out, break them, try again, and, ultimately get it right. A minute later, the music finished and they unveiled their drivable WMD. And whatever it was, I wanted one.

Same with *The Karate Kid* and *Rocky*. And *Rocky II*. And *Rocky III*. And all of the rest of the *Rockys*. These guys were up against the wall, something had to change. It was time to learn how to kick some ass. The music starts pumping. They try things. Fail. Try some more. Get better. Get even better. A minute later, the music fades out and they're transformed. That's the montage.

The Hollywood montage speeds us through the challenging, less sexy part of growth and learning — the suck, the work, the trial and error. The montage feeds us the expectation that the learning process is quick and easy. But that's where most of us allow ourselves to get beaten by resistance.

When I'm coaching a guy and he's telling me about some big challenge in his life — learning how to expand his business, learning how to have difficult conversations with his family, whatever — I like to remind him of the montage.

This is the part in the movie where we dig deep and *learn* something. This is where we *grow* to meet the challenge. This is where we get to practice and screw up and figure out how to get it right.

So let's ask ourselves: If we're going to overcome this challenge, what would our montage look like? What would we need to practice and learn and create in order to tackle this challenge?

And most importantly, we have to ask, What song will I play?

Let's crank it up and get to work.

Now that we've put our excuses in their place, we're going to be leaning into discomfort. And to do this, we're going to learn how to own our power — without being a dick.

Free Bonus

Take advantage of the free video guide I've created for *This Book Will Make You Dangerous*. Each chapter includes a video and PDF to help you save time and energy.

Get it for free by visiting:
TrippLanier.com/Bonus

CHAPTER 5:
Be Bold — Lean into Discomfort and Develop Self-Leadership

When we revisit the fears that keep us stuck in a prey mentality, we're considering the idea that our primitive, survival-obsessed brains are constantly asking:

What do I do so that I'm not uncomfortable?
What do I do so that I don't risk losing something I care about?
What do I do so that I don't look like a jackass?

Which means that, if we're unconsciously going through our day, we're giving our power over to a part of us that believes it will *die* if it's uncomfortable.

Sounds crazy, but let's roll with it. Let's imagine that we're dying.

Let's Die Right Now

Do me a favor. Wherever you are right now, tilt your head up and stare at the ceiling for a minute. It sounds weird, but just do it. Get a good look. Take it in because chances are you'll have a similar view in the last moments of your life as you lay on the ground or on a stretcher or a hospital bed somewhere. This is the view you will likely have during your last few breaths.

Let's go further. Let's imagine these *are* the last moments of your life. And while it may be a drag to reach the end of the road, are you at peace with how you're living your life now? When you're faced with the certainty of your own death, do you feel aligned with how you're choosing to live your life today? When you're in touch with your mortality, are you more aware of what you're waiting to do, what you're tolerating, what you're denying yourself? When you're in touch with the reality that you will most definitely die, are you able to find the peace of mind that comes from knowing your actions are in alignment with what you truly care about?

No matter what, the clock keeps on ticking and we get closer and closer to this moment where we're staring at the ceiling taking our final breaths. There's nothing we can do about that. But we can use our mortality as a healthy way to get out of our small and limited thinking right now. We can use our inevitable death to find a sweet spot where we *play* for what we want while also not taking anything too seriously. We can use it as encouragement to align our lives with freedom, aliveness, love, and peace.

The good news is that we don't have to wait for a terminal diagnosis to get out of the rat race. We don't have to wait for anyone to give us permission. We don't have to wait until we're *enough* in the eyes of our inner critic or anyone else.

We never know when our time will be up, so why be dead now? Let's live. Let's be bold. And to do that we're going to own our *power*.

Power and Maturity

Power can get a bad rap in our culture, and understandably so. To put it lightly, throughout history, those in power have often used it to diminish others. Millions of people have been enslaved and killed in the name of power for another ruler, religion, or country. And it's often those who feel powerless that act out with sex or violence in a feeble attempt to *become* powerful.

When power is misunderstood, we tend to see it as a zero-sum game. Meaning, if someone gets more powerful, it's because someone else had to give up their power. And this creates an interesting situation for men — who, let's face it, have been the supreme dickheads on this planet. Hands down. So is the solution to hand over our balls and spine and back hair, just so the world can be a more peaceful place?

I don't believe so. Giving up our power is still playing into that fear-based, zero-sum game. I believe the world's a much better place when we — you, me, all of us on the planet — learn how to co-create and own our power with *maturity*.

When we own our power with maturity, we treat others the way we would want to be treated. We stop treating others like primitive, crack-sniffing apes who worry about being the "alpha." We stop the gossiping and trash-talking about others so that we can feel superior. We stop using others as simply a stepping stone to get what we want. We stop assuming our neighbors and fellow countrymen are adversaries just because they don't look like us or vote the same way that we do.

It's when we believe our own fear-based-group-think-fever-dream that we feel justified to ruin reputations, relationships, and revenue streams. And nobody is immune. This primitive practice of exerting power *over* others happens on the left and the right — in back alleys, bedrooms, and boardrooms.

Again — it's our outdated, primitive mindset that has us justify doing terrible things to one another in the name of "survival." And when this mindset has us believe that our cushy, egoic "success" is at stake, then we feel justified to be *aggressive* — to smear and lie or even kill.

But if we take a minute to examine the beliefs used to justify tearing others down, most of the time, we'll see that we're just being hijacked by fear.

What do I do so that I'm not uncomfortable?
What do I do so that I don't risk losing something I care about?
What do I do so that I don't get kicked out of the group?

When hijacked by this primitive pattern, we're just perpetuating the same zero-sum "kill or be killed" game, even though we're nowhere near mortal danger. While it may seem beneficial in the short term, this approach sows seeds of future casualties on both sides. It kills our peace of mind. It robs us of the opportunity to experience the deeply rewarding meaning that comes from creating alliances that build others up.

And this makes us weak.

Expanding Our Options

So what does this look like on a personal level? How can we tell if we're misusing our power?

We feel trapped.
We feel drained.
We feel isolated or alone.
We feel stressed out or bored.

Whether we're fed up with our relationships or professions or whatever, we continue to tolerate stress and overwhelm and boredom, because we believe we don't have any options that are immune to loss. So we play not to lose.

In order to avoid this discomfort — this tension — we're creating a life or relationship or career based on what we *think* we can get. In order to minimize risk, we play it safe and only see the opportunities we believe are a *sure thing*. But think about it — how much of our lives can truly be a sure thing? Very, very little. Which means that when we play not to lose, we focus only on the things we think we can get, and we limit our options — our power — immensely.

Here's an example. Years ago, as a new coach, I was working too much, not earning enough, and wondering what the hell was wrong with me. *Why can't I be happy? Do I need to go to therapy? Do I need to learn how to get better at tolerating crap?*

At the time, it didn't occur to me that I could raise my fees and work less. Why? Because I was so afraid of taking a loss. It felt too risky. Playing not to lose kept me focused only on what was a sure thing. It kept me from even considering the possibilities that would strengthen me and my family. In that situation, I didn't need therapy. My coach helped me see that I just needed to practice being bold, deliver higher value, and raise my fees. Through experience, I learned that I'd still be fine even if a few people told me no.

So, as we go forward, we want to keep in mind that immense power is available to us when we're willing to take on some discomfort and risk from time to time. Because when we're willing to be bold and own our power with maturity…

We no longer tolerate vast amounts of drama because we're willing to speak up and co-create what we want, instead of automatically assuming we'll be rejected.

We no longer believe we have "productivity issues" because we focus on what's truly important. We stop distracting ourselves with the small stuff and become far more effective.

We let go of the scarcity habit of trying to carry six gallons in a five-gallon bucket. We challenge the idea that we can never get "enough." We learn to create what truly nourishes us, instead of striving to fill our lives with stuff that just makes us weak.

And we can do this in a way that aligns with our sense of freedom, aliveness, love, and peace of mind. Which means we're going to want to grow up.

Inner Authority — Clarifying What You Want

Forty-Five-Year-Old Boys

As infants, we were helpless and completely dependent upon someone else for everything we needed. We were powerless to do anything except cry when we wanted something. We felt discomfort from a poopy diaper or a hunger pain or a burp or too many blankets or not enough blankets. We felt that tension, and we did the only thing we could do — we made a big racket and then someone fumbled around. They played a guessing game to try and figure out what we wanted and then bring it to us so that we'd shut up.

Does he need a fresh diaper? More milk? Is he too hot? Too cold? Maybe I should have pulled out.

Regardless, back in the day, all we had to do was complain in order to have someone take care of our desires. It was that caregiver who stepped into the role of authority, to take the lead and clarify what was wanted. And it was the caregiver who owned the responsibility, the power, to be the one to take effective action so the desire was met.

Those are two key points right there — (1) clarifying what is wanted and (2) taking ownership or responsibility.

Now, folks grow up physically but many never really outgrow this immature way of trying to get what they want in life. This is how we end up with boys walking around in the bodies of grown men. Let's not kid ourselves here either — there are quite a few princesses out there walking around in the bodies of grown women, too.

Whether they're conscious of it or not, they still believe that their happiness is someone else's responsibility. If they're not happy, then it must be their wife or job or the government or the media or "those people" who are to blame. And when they're stuck in this immature place, they never really learn how to take ownership of their experience. They spend more time criticizing and complaining and pointing out what they don't want instead of (1) clarifying what they do want and (2) taking responsibility to create what they want for themselves.

That's because making the effort to clarify what we want and take responsibility is *uncomfortable*. If we're committed to avoiding discomfort and risk, then it's seemingly much easier to look for someone else to handle the burden of our well-being.

Here. This is hard. You deal with it.

But that's how children respond. We're not children. We're adults. Complaining and protesting may give us a sense of short-term righteousness. Handing over the responsibility of our burden may give us a moment of illusory relief. But remember this — what we perceive to be a burden is actually our power.

Let's be clear — we want to be integrated. We want a *healthy*, vibrant little kid inside of us so that we can experience all that life has to offer. But he's not the guy to put in charge of running our adult world of relationships and careers and bills to pay. We need to approach our sense of authority and power from a more mature stance.

Take Your Stance: Choose to Be an Adult

When we're unconscious, we rely on an *external* sense of authority for direction — comparisons, expectations, following the herd, rebelling against the herd. This means we often fall into the habit of protecting, pleasing, and proving to determine our life choices.

I'll say it again. Comfort, safety, and acceptance aren't limiting — until they are. But when we put our needs to protect and please and prove in check, then we can step into self-leadership aligned with strength. We can harness our *internal* authority to ask questions like...

What will truly strengthen me beyond just being successful?
What do I want beyond the options I'm expected to take?
What do I stand for, even if it might not jive with those around me?
Who am I really, beyond just trying to fit in?

And to do this we need to make a very conscious choice:

Am I going to create my life as a wounded, fearful child?
Or am I going to create my life as an empowered adult?

In other words, am I going to buy into some hogwash story that I can't tolerate small amounts of discomfort or risk? Am I going to be eclipsed by the belief that I can't withstand a few odd looks or comments from others?

Or am I going to recognize that what I truly want — to have a stronger, more expansive experience of life — means that I'll feel a little discomfort from time to time? Am I going to recognize that I'm a full-grown adult and I can learn how to handle this stuff?

Choosing to be an adult means we're choosing to be allies of ourselves. We're going to drop the complaining and bitching and take full responsibility for our experience. And because we're being adults, it also means that we're going to challenge the idea that our lover or family or job or community are somehow our adversaries — the things that block our ability to experience freedom, aliveness, love, and peace. As adults, we're going to be allies to others and seek ways to co-create solutions, instead of choosing to betray ourselves or attack anyone who gets in our way.

So that we no longer sound like an infant wailing in the night, let's learn how to turn our protests into solutions.

Protesting Doesn't Solve Problems. Solutions Do.

As infants, we may have learned that putting up a big fuss got someone else's attention. They'd hear us cry and take care of us. That was a good thing. That was healthy. Unfortunately, the habit of complaining — by itself — doesn't create the solutions to our problems.

No matter how much we fuss and whine and point out what we don't like, it still doesn't answer one very simple, powerful question:

Well, if I don't like XYZ, then what do I want?

When we catch ourselves blaming or complaining, the quickest way to bounce out of the habit is to ask ourselves this question. Immediately, it challenges us to pivot out of a limiting mindset into a powerful one. It challenges us to take responsibility for *ourselves* and start looking for solutions.

This simple question can be so powerful that it can confuse us. Specificity can help, so let's throw out a few variations that can get the creative juices flowing …

What would I want if I knew it would be easy and fun?
What would I want if I knew I wouldn't waste my time or energy or money?
What would I want if I knew no one would get hurt or upset?
What would I want if I knew no one would think I was being weird?
What would I want if I wasn't so worried about screwing up?

These questions help us see what we may want beyond our need to protect and please and prove. Eventually, we may even choose to use the answers to these questions to figure out what actions to take next.

Oh Shit! What Does This Mean?

I've had many, many of these conversations with men over the years, and there's often a very real fear that comes with clarifying what we want. We worry that if we expose what we want — even just to ourselves — that it'll somehow snowball out of control. We make our desires mean something, and it doesn't take long for our brains to freak out and create a worst-case scenario.

I want to spend more time outside of my business. Oh shit! Does that mean I'll lose control if I'm not there sixty hours per week?

I want to spend more time doing things just for myself outside of my family. Oh shit! Does that mean my kids are going to hate me for the rest of my life?

I want to put my mouth on my wife's super-hot friend. Oh shit! Does that mean I'm a terrible husband and I don't love my wife anymore?

It doesn't take much for our primitive threat-assessment device to turn these desires into some story that means our lives are going to fall apart. But let's remember that we're highly complex, emotional beings. We are filled with confusing contradictions. Just because we want something on Wednesday doesn't mean it'll still be true on Friday. As adults, we can recognize that there's a massive amount of daylight between our desires and the choices we make.

What's more likely is that once we dig out that unmet desire and let it simply be, we usually feel an amazing amount of peace. Just giving ourselves permission to clarify what we want, we may start to realize that it's not so awful or crazy or reckless or dangerous. We may start to see how others have created this in their own lives, how others have faced this challenge in a way that empowered them. Once we give ourselves permission to own what we want for ourselves we may begin to challenge the very idea that we — or anyone we care about — are in any danger at all.

So here's a suggestion, how about for now, as we go through this process together, we simply say, "Okay. At this specific time on this specific day I wanted XYZ." That's it. That's all. No big deal. For now, it doesn't have to *mean* anything. We can simply observe it as just another thought, another cloud in the sky passing by.

How's that sound?

Later on, we'll learn how to bring more discernment to our inner authority, so that we don't become impulsive hedonists. But for now, we just want to give ourselves permission to express ourselves freely *to just ourselves*.[7] We don't have to do anything with this information yet.

A Pain in the Ass is Valuable Information

Many times, we have a hard time clarifying what we want because we're focused on outcomes instead of experiences. In fact, we get so focused on external *things* — dollar amounts, stuff we want to buy, our weight on the scale — that we completely forget about our subjective, emotional experience. And this can be quite dangerous if this internal *experience* is trying to send us an important message.

You know when you're driving down the interstate and you take a look out the window at that billboard for that sketchy trucker strip club that also sells beach towels by the pound and then you hear and feel that JUBBAJUBBAJUBBAJUBBAJUBBAJUBBAJUBBA!!! That's the *experience* of your car running over those little asphalt bumps on the edge of the road. They're uncomfortable. They're loud. And they're *meant* to be that way. They're *meant* to get your attention because they're trying to

---

7 A private journal can be helpful to track what we want and see what is consistent and what changes over time.

guide you to stay on the road. That feedback was unpleasant, but it was necessary to wake you up and get you back in the moment so that you could course-correct. It was a pain in the ass for a good reason.

Well, what if the other uncomfortable experiences in our lives — feeling bored or stressed or drained or trapped or isolated — could be used to give us similar information? If we don't like the way we feel, what if we didn't choose to dismiss or numb or distract ourselves from that feeling? Like those groovy asphalt bumps on the side of the road, what if these pain in the ass experiences could serve as a guidance system to wake us up, bring us into the moment, and help us course-correct to make better choices?

If we want to learn how to connect with our inner authority, then we want to put down the bong, turn off the screens, take a break from work, and get present. Slow down. Reconnect with ourselves. In this moment. We want to check in with our current experience, our inner dashboard, and see where we're feeling the opposite:

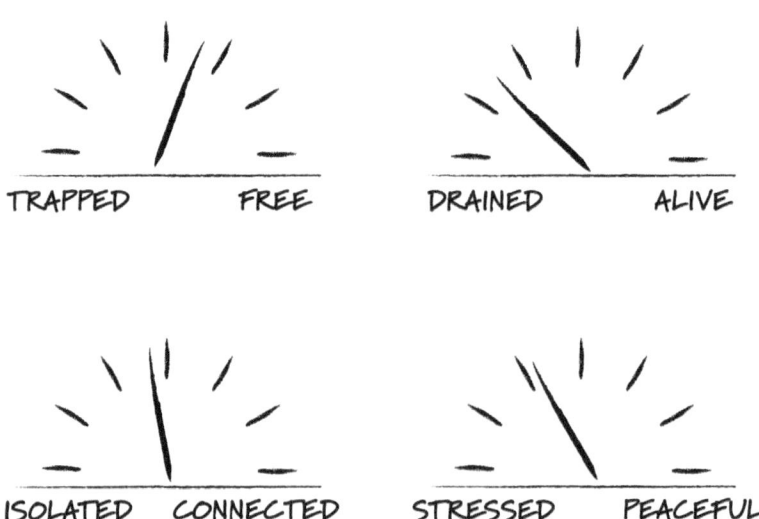

Instead of freedom, where am I feeling trapped?
Instead of aliveness, where am I feeling drained?
Instead of love and connection, where am I feeling alone or isolated?
Instead of peace, where am I feeling stressed or bored?

Now, instead of medicating ourselves or running away from the stuff that doesn't feel good, we can get curious. We can view this pain in the ass as the *doorway* to clarifying the experiences we do want.

If I'm feeling trapped, then what would have me feel more free today?
If I'm feeling drained, then what would have me feel more alive today?
If I'm feeling isolated, then what would have me feel more connected and loved today?
If I'm feeling stressed out or bored, then what would have me feel more at peace today?

Now, here's the deal ... we don't want to be like that moron at the gym who thinks he's going to turn around seven years of sitting on the couch in one afternoon. Pick *one* area and just focus there. Start small. Go slow. Stretching and pushing ourselves too much and too quickly is a recipe for misery and anxiety.

So let's talk about anxiety.

Use Anxiety to Clarify What You Want

Anxiety is an awful experience, and it tends to surround the areas of our lives that matter most — our relationships, health, and finances.

I interviewed Chip Conley a while back. He's taken his years of entrepreneurship and turned them into a few powerful, practical books. One of these is called *Emotional Equations*, and in that book, Conley breaks down anxiety into a simple mathematical equation that looks like this:

Anxiety = Uncertainty x Powerlessness

Right. Okay. So, what the hell does that mean? He's basically saying that when our uncertainty is combined with a sense of powerlessness, it explodes into a much larger experience of anxiety. To take our anxiety head on, he recommends doing a simple exercise called the "Anxiety Balance Sheet." And we can use it right now to reduce our anxiety by clarifying what we want to do next and stepping into power.

Ready?

So think of an area of your life that's giving you anxiety. Grab that journal or whatever you like to write with, and create four lists answering the following questions with regards to this specific situation:

What do I know?
What don't I know?
What's within my power?
What's outside of my power?

When we take a few minutes to answer these questions thoughtfully a few things typically emerge. One, we're giving ourselves a headache worrying about stuff that's way outside of our control. Two, we tend to know more about a situation than we had previously assumed. And three, we can quickly reclaim our sense of authority and power by getting answers to the questions we haven't answered yet.[8]

If I'm spinning my wheels, freaking out about XYZ, then my anxiety tells me that some certainty will minimize it. Instead of burying my head in the sand, where can I find that answer? Who can I ask about this? What action can I take?

---

[8] Explore this idea further by checking out my interview with Chip Conley on The New Man Podcast.

Within minutes, we can step out of powerlessness into action. We can be on the computer or in direct communication with someone who knows about this problem. Instead of self-medicating or trying to distract ourselves, we can get curious. Instead of running away from our anxiety, we can learn to steer directly into it.

These simple questions and practices are just a few ways that we can shift our focus away from external authority (saying, "*Just tell me what to do*," making comparisons to others, meeting expectations) to an internal sense of authority (asking, *What are my experiences telling me? What will have me feel stronger, more free, alive, loving, and at peace?*).

Now that we're getting a sense of (1) what we want, let's talk about how we can (2) take responsibility.

Taking Responsibility for What You Want

So what are we taking away so far?

If we're willing to make the effort, then we can develop our sense of authority — our self-leadership. Instead of reacting to challenges as our scared, wounded child, we can practice approaching our lives as a mature adult. We can learn to catch ourselves complaining and bitching and protesting, and immediately pivot by asking, "Well, if I don't want this, then what *do* I want?" We can give ourselves the space and permission to freely express our desires to ourselves without needing to judge them or freak out. And then we can learn to use our "negative" experiences as information — as a doorway to reveal what it is that we do want.

These are some very basic, simple ways for us to practice stepping into our authority. And while clarifying what we want is essential, it's only part of the process. If we're looking at the metaphorical dinner menu of life, and we don't like the options listed on the page, then who says we have to settle for what's written down? If we're no longer lit up by our options, it's usually because we're playing defense, we're *playing not to lose*, we're avoiding a no, we're only pursuing the options that we think we can get.

But just because something isn't written on the menu of life doesn't mean it isn't available. If we're willing to relax our constant need to protect and please and prove, then what's to stop us from being bold and asking for what we want? What if we lived our lives as if we knew "The Chef" personally?

My schooling is a joke, and it's not preparing me for the profession I want. Instead of huffing and puffing and complaining, what if I designed my own education?

I'm really happy in the company where I work, but I've got so much more to offer. Instead of going with the flow, who can I talk to about stepping into a bigger role?

I love my partner, but I'm getting bored with our sex life. What do I want to suggest that would make it more exciting?

As part of my work with coaching clients, I challenge them on a regular basis to (1) clarify what they want and (2) take responsibility. We practice being bold and testing out our fears and assumptions just like building any other kind of skill. We make it a game to go into seemingly "threatening" situations out in the real world and ask for stuff we're absolutely *certain* will get us rejected. I play along, too. Here are just a handful of some of the things we've done together:

- Go into a restaurant and ask them for items on your grocery list (this worked up to a point)
- Go into a burrito joint and ask if you can make your own burrito (this got rejected)
- Double your professional fees (this works more often than you'd think)

- Ask hotels and airlines for free upgrades (this, too, works more often than you'd think)
- Walk around a mall asking random people to take selfies with you (also works way more often than you'd think)

Regardless of the activity, after confronting our fears and practicing our ability to boldly ask for what we want, we learn three big things:

Number one, most of the time people say yes. In many cases they're happy to help with such unconventional requests because it makes their day more interesting, too. It's inspiring to be around people who own what they want. This can be mind-blowing for those of us who believe the limiting voice in our heads. *Aw shucks. I don't want to make anybody uncomfortable.*

Number two, we feel more energized and expansive because we begin to see — from experience — that our reality is much different than our fears would have us believe. We begin to see — from experience — that the world has way more possibilities than limitations.

And number three, we begin to train ourselves to be with the tension and discomfort that arises as we approach the edge of our comfort zone.

Whatever the situation may be, it's all the same. Stepping outside of our comfort zone is, by definition, going to be uncomfortable. Period. Whether that action is asking for a larger dinner portion or asking our partners to consider moving across the country to start a new life, this is how we practice facing our fears and resistance.

Like a basketball player may shoot free throws, by practicing this regularly, we forge new pathways in our brain. Instead of reinforcing all of the fear-based nightmares running through our minds, we learn to steer directly into our fears in service of owning what we want. Doing this regularly means that when the bigger challenges show up, we're prepared to address them from a position of strength. *I know this feeling. I've got this.*

Often, what we want is totally doable — it's just not obvious. It's not what others in the herd are choosing. If we can't figure out what we want in life because we don't like the options, then let's learn to create more options. And if we've practiced being bold, then we know our options far outweigh our limitations.

So how would your life expand if, every day, you practiced asking for something you believed you couldn't have? How would your life be different if getting a "no" was no big deal? Practice being bold and willing to get a "no" every day, and you'll be amazed at how strong you become.

Expect Pushback

As we discussed earlier, if our entire lives have been designed to avoid discomfort, risk, and looking like a pork sword, then everything and everyone in our lives is there because it supports us in staying exactly where we are. Owning what we want is going to disrupt that balance. So let's expect a few bumps in the road. Let's expect to get a bit of pushback.

Wait, you wanna do what? What has gotten into you?

Pushback doesn't mean that what we want is necessarily bad or wrong. It just means we're stepping outside of the norm. Consider it a test. *How much do I want this?*

This is why starting small helps us get used to these little challenges, these little tests when we choose to be bold. We learn to expect the raised eyebrows and the weird looks and the turbulence. We learn to expect that a few feathers may get a little ruffled. But that doesn't mean we need to abandon what we want — or be a jerk about it, either.

Now, as the stakes are raised and we begin to be bold in ways that are more impactful to others, we're going to experience greater pushback. And that's where we're going to confront the one little word that will keep us playing small.

No.

That one can sting. Call it what you want — rejection, failure, or getting owned — many of us have designed our entire lives to avoid it. The "no" could come from a lover, our "target market," or anyone all the way up to some judgy guy with a white beard and Birkenstocks who lives on top of a cloud. But most of the time, the "no" comes from within. It comes from ourselves. And because we're so highly attuned to rejection, we typically defend in one of two ways when we are challenged.

Collapse or Posture

"No" is a force so powerful that for many, just getting a whiff of a "no" means we'll immediately go into a defensive mode.

There's no freakin' way I could talk to that best-selling author about collaborating on a project.
There's no freakin' way I could change lanes professionally without taking a drop in pay.
There's no freakin' way I could take a weekend with the guys without my wife throwing a fit.

That doesn't sound too powerful, does it?

The first way we typically defend ourselves against the probability of a "no" is to *collapse*. This is where we just give up. We make excuses. We don't even allow ourselves to want something because we've already convinced ourselves that it's going to rock the boat.

Sorry, guys. Uh, something came up. I'm just not gonna be able to make it this weekend. Maybe next time.

This happens because we're usually very *open* and considerate to others, but quick to sell ourselves out. And while our desire to make sure we don't ruffle any feathers may seem considerate, it's usually far more selfish. According to Dr. Robert Glover, who wrote *No More Mr. Nice Guy*, it's because when others are uncomfortable, we feel uncomfortable. So by bending over backwards and playing the chameleon, we manage and control what others feel so that we don't have to experience our own tension and discomfort.[9]

The second way we may typically respond to the probability of a "no" is to *posture*. This is where we bulldoze.

It's my way or the highway, babe. I'm going. I don't care what you say.

When we're posturing, we're so *firm* in what we want that we dismiss the impact we're having on others. Posturing means we puff ourselves up to shield ourselves from the pushback. We close off our compassion and concern so that we don't have to feel the discomfort that comes from seeing things from another perspective. We bulldoze over others before they have the opportunity to push us around.

But like collapsing, it's just a defense. Collapsing and posturing are both rooted in insecurity and fear and avoidance instead of strength and creativity. One has us betray ourselves, while the other has us betray our genuine concern for others. They both lead to toxicity, resentment, and isolation. And they both kill our peace of mind.[10]

The good news is that we don't have to stay stuck in this duality of being *either* open or firm.

---

9 Be sure to listen to my interview with Dr. Robert Glover who wrote *No More Mr. Nice Guy*. He does a great job of explaining the "nice guy syndrome" I'm describing here.

10 Thanks to Decker Cunov and his work with regards to posture/collapse.

Be Open *and* Firm

When we practice being open *and* firm, we stay open to the impact our actions may have while also staying firm in what we want.

I'm excited about this trip with the guys, and I want to go. I also imagine this may impact you and the kids in some way, so let's discuss that. If I choose to go away on this trip, how will it impact you? What could we co-create so that there's less of a burden on you?

When we're open and firm, we're open to hearing how we may impact others while still staying firm in our desire. We're not asking for permission like some child, but we are showing our concern. We're in a frame of mind to create solutions instead of getting bogged down in right or wrong, justifying or explaining.

And this is because we see ourselves as responsible for our own happiness and others as responsible for their own. When we take our stance as an adult in our relationships, we stop treating our wives as if they're our mothers or some little girl who needs to be rescued. When we take our stance as an adult in the world, we see others as peers, as partners, as people who are co-creating this life with us instead of victims or villains who get in our way. This keeps us from sneaking around like teenagers who deceive the people they care about most. This keeps us from falling into the trap of believing it's our job to play Superman to everyone around us, too.[11] This ensures that we live with integrity and treat others the way that we would want to be treated.

Regardless, at the core of this way of living is our willingness to step into discomfort instead of striving so hard to avoid it.

---

[11] Be sure to check out my video where I discuss The Drama Triangle which was developed by Stephen Karpman. Also check out my interview with David Emerald where we discuss ways to move out of drama by using The Empowerment Dynamic.

Expand Your Capacity for Discomfort

Tough Guys and a Room Full of Flaccid Dicks

Years ago, I was in a men's group out in Boulder with a fantastic group of guys. One of them was an older fella with a lot of experience facilitating men's workshops around the world. We revolved group leadership each week, and when it was his turn to take the helm, he'd always invite us to take off our clothes and sit in the circle naked.

Oh. Look at you right now. Sitting there imagining a bunch of dudes sitting in a circle naked talking about their feelings and stuff. You probably want more information, huh? Okay. That guy leading had a freakin' baby arm for a penis. He needed a winch to get that dong-hog back in his drawers. And it's cold in Boulder. Often. And I'll be honest — this put me at a disadvantage because, you know, my penis isn't in the league of dong-hogs.

So, how are you feeling right now? When I would tell my so-called "tough guy" friends about my naked men's group meetings, their eyes would go wide and their mouths would drop open. It was like I just told them that I had eaten an entire ostrich.

Wait. You did WHAT with a bunch of other dudes?

These guys — conditioned to make sure they didn't do anything sissy or "gay" — would rather jump over a pit of poisonous snakes rather than sit in a room with a bunch of exposed, flaccid dicks.

But let's be clear, in this scenario dicks aren't really the threat — even that one that was as big as a river otter. So then, what is it that we really fear?

What We Really Fear is a Feeling

Let's say we've got a sense of what we want, and now we're in the creative process to make it happen. It's time to get bold, and that's when we can expect resistance to kick in. We want to run away, and here come the justifications.

Most of us will describe *outcomes* like "failure" or "running out of money" or "getting trapped in a situation." Those sound like solid, logical reasons for why we want to bail, but they're not quite the truth.

Let's remember — our minds have a tendency to imagine outcomes and then immediately assume what those experiences might feel like. Some may imagine having a pile of money and assume that will *feel* great. Others imagine screwing up a presentation and assume that will *feel* devastating.

Our aversion to tension is different for each of us. Maybe it's being in a room full of naked men. I know guys that won't take the elevator because they don't want to have to make small talk with a stranger. It's not the small talk they fear, it's the uncomfortable *feeling* they have when they're with someone they don't know. And I've coached military veterans who would seemingly prefer to go into a life-threatening situation rather than *experience* the discomfort that shows up when they sit down with their wives to discuss the fate of their marriage.

Bottom line — underneath the event or outcome itself, is a feeling we most want to avoid. And for the sake of this conversation, let's keep things super simple and call that uncomfortable feeling *tension*.

Tension comes in many forms. As testosterone-crazed, horny teenagers, we may have experienced tension when we got turned on. It may have been so intense and so uncomfortable that we trained ourselves to "release" this tension through ejaculation as quickly as possible. And if we've continued to build a life designed to avoid discomfort, then we may still believe tension is a signal that something needs to be expelled from the body. We may still believe that tension means something is wrong.

But what if that wasn't true?

I grew up freediving and spearfishing in the Florida Keys. I had zero training other than watching my dad. As humans, when we hold our breath for a long time, there's a point where our diaphragms start to involuntarily contract or spasm. It's natural. And when I was a teenager looking for dinner under the rocks twenty-five feet below the surface, I was convinced these uncomfortable spasms meant that I was about to black out and die. I *believed* that these were my last gasps. Scary stuff.

Fast forward to the time I finally took a freediving course, and I learned that those involuntary contractions meant that I was nowhere near blacking out. Our instructor[12] told us that those first few contractions were a good indicator that we were roughly *halfway* towards our breath-holding limit. In other words — even though there was a lot of tension and discomfort — I wasn't about to die *in that moment*. Regardless of what I believed, I was capable of so much more even if there was tension.

So what if this was true in other areas of our lives? Many times, our experience of tension has us *convinced* that we're at our edge. *I can't take any more!* But if we're willing to develop our awareness, if we're willing to experiment, then we can expand our capacity to be with tension. We can learn that we don't have to bail just because we may encounter a bit of discomfort. We can learn to be far more bold than we may have previously believed.

Let's try it out. Let's see.

---

[12] Special thanks to Sam Blount of Frontline Freediving.

Test Your Capacity for Physical Tension

If we want to expand our capacity to experience tension, then we first need to become aware of the part of us that wants to avoid discomfort altogether. We want to be able to recognize this form of resistance and its excuses and limiting beliefs. This takes practice, so let's go through a couple of simple, very safe practices that we can use to dial up the tension and build awareness of our resistance.

First up, let's talk about *physical* tension.

Grab a big-ass bowl from your kitchen and fill it with a bunch of ice and some cold water. Grab a timer and then roll up your sleeve. Yeah, I'm serious. We're doing this.

Start the timer, slide your hand into the ice, and then notice how long it takes for that voice in your head to say, *Uh uhn. I've had enough of this so-called "experiment." I can't take anymore. I'm out!* Notice the time, but don't pull your hand out yet. Keep it in. Breathe. Breathe in and out very deeply. Give yourself permission to make noise because it helps to move that tension, that energy.

Now, instead of distracting yourself, get curious. Just witness the voice that wants to convince you that you will get frostbite and need to have your hand amputated. If possible, put even more attention on the feeling itself. What is it? Is it an ache? A tingling? Where is it exactly? Is it on the skin or is it in your bones? What do you actually feel? How does it change over time? Do you adapt to the tension?

You can obviously take your hand out at any time, but most importantly, stay aware of that voice in your head that's committed to keeping you *physically* comfortable. What kind of stuff does it tell you? How does it try to convince you to bail? And when you take your hand out, look at the timer. Notice the gap between the point your mind told you to pull your hand out and when you chose to do it. How much longer were you able to keep your hand in the ice after that voice tried to convince you that you couldn't handle anymore?

Now let's be really clear. When we've given up our power, we try to find ways to tolerate more bullshit. And there is certainly a tension associated with tolerating bullshit — it's called boredom and overwhelm. But I don't want to help you get better at tolerating bullshit. In fact, tolerating bullshit is an indicator that we're avoiding *emotional* tension. So let's switch gears and do another experiment.

Test Your Capacity for Emotional Tension

Put away the phone and shut down the screens and turn off the music and get rid of any distractions. Find a comfortable sitting position where you can sit upright — no slouching or lying down. Start a timer and then just sit there *without moving*. Just watch your thoughts as if you were watching a movie. And, like the ice experiment, it won't take long until tension arises. But instead of reacting or struggling against it or distracting ourselves, we can simply witness it. We can get curious. We can notice the excuses that pop up, the justifications we manufacture for ditching the experiment.

This is a waste of time. Wait a second. Oh, right. You forgot to send a message about that thing. You better go do that now.

Take note of the time, and then simply witness this part of us — our resistance — work its magic. If this is uncomfortable, get curious about the discomfort. Is it boredom? Loneliness? When you slow down enough to actually be with yourself, is it scary? There's nothing to change or shift — just notice the emotions and thoughts that have you feeling uncomfortable. Notice when you want to go up in your head to explain and justify and defend. If possible, just come back to the experience in your body.

What am I feeling? How is it changing from moment to moment?

Again, you can keep going as long as you wish. And if you keep going, you may notice that a sense of calm and peace eventually arises. But regardless of what happens, be sure to recognize that there was a gap between the moment your resistance said *enough!* and when you actually chose to end the experiment.

This experiment — which is really just a form of meditation — gives us an opportunity to experience our emotional tension and witness that voice within us that wants to resist it. Because here's the deal — that voice is living within you, me, all of us 24/7. It's constantly telling us to avoid discomfort and tension. This is the voice that, when left unchecked, will convince us that we can't handle even a *little bit* of tension. It'll convince us that we can't be bold. It'll keep us playing small.

Get to know this voice, because it's never going away.

The good news is that we can practice this daily. We can find small, safe ways to confront our resistance to tension and expand our capacity to be with it. This is how we build confidence. This is how we empower ourselves to steer directly into the discomfort that arises when we own what we want in service of greater freedom, aliveness, love, and peace.

I know this is going to be uncomfortable. I know that there will be a voice that tells me to quit. And I know that I can handle it.

Now let's explore how it's much easier to be bold and relieve our tension when we put our challenges into perspective.

What We Want — or Fear — Has Three Parts

After we clarify what we want and engage the bold process of creating, we're going to encounter resistance. Resistance often convinces us that we're standing on the edge of a diving platform high above the water. Resistance convinces us that the next step is really a leap.

Ugh. What have I gotten myself into? I don't think I can do this.

Most often this is where we drain ourselves and get stuck because we can only see our challenge from one perspective instead of three. So let's break down our challenge into its three main parts.

The first part happens *before* we take the scary step. This is the worry and anxiety and dread. Like a scared child frozen out on the end of the diving board, we're usually in a state of anxiety. *I don't know what's going to happen. I don't know what I should do.* We can spend months or years or decades frozen in this place of fearful anticipation and worst-case scenarios.

The second part is when we get into action. This happens when we engage our challenge. And weirdly enough, when we're engaged, we don't usually feel the fear anymore. If anything we begin to experience engagement — aliveness. If our challenge and our skill levels are aligned, we may even begin to experience *flow*.[13] Like the kid who just stepped off of the diving board and into the air, while we're in the act of creating, we're focused on the challenge itself. In that moment, we're not making up scary stories about the future, because we're in the present, getting stuff done.

And the third part is the realization that occurs after we tackle our challenge. We're no longer that scared, frozen kid trapped inside his head. We're transformed as a result of going through our challenge and coming out the other side. At a minimum, we're simply relieved to be done with the thing, but most likely, we experience a sense of peace. We're no longer burdened by the belief that we have to escape this ordeal. We're now stronger and empowered. Maybe we're already running to get back in line so that we can do it again. *Hey! Slow down! No running at the pool!*

---

[13] To learn more about flow, check out my interviews with Steven Kotler (*The Rise of Superman*) and Jamie Wheal (Flow Genome Project) on The New Man Podcast.

So what can we take away from this? The first part — that anxious, anticipatory stage — is by far the worst. That's where we typically experience the greatest discomfort. If we take the time to review our previous experiences, we can see that waiting to do something feels quite different than the experience of actually doing it. But we don't have to buy into the idea that just because this first part is so uncomfortable then the whole thing is going to be uncomfortable. When we understand that this first stage is the worst, then we can choose to act quickly to relieve that tension. We can choose to be bold, to step into power, and engage our challenges sooner rather than later.

Taking the Teeth Out of Tension

Aligning our lives with what strengthens us requires us to own our power. This means we take our stance as an adult, step into our own sense of inner authority, and do the work to clarify what we want. But we don't stop there. We then take responsibility for creating what we want. And to do this, we learn to expand our capacity for greater physical and emotional discomfort. Instead of running away from tension, we learn how to let it inform us and guide us to greater expansion.

By practicing this bold, powerful way of living, we don't wait for permission or opportunities to show up. We create those opportunities. Instead of engaging in power struggles with others, we invite them to co-create with us. When we relax our need to protect and please and prove, we drop the belief that we can't say no to what drains us. We create what we want from this empowered place instead of hoping that *one day* we'll somehow finally get permission to have what we want.

Now that we've addressed our commitment to avoiding discomfort, let's talk about how we can strengthen our ability to take risks — and maybe even have some fun in the process.

CHAPTER 6:
Be Playful — Minimize Risk and Create on Your Terms

All right, let's reconnect with those three fear-based questions that keep us on in a prey mentality:

What do I do so that I'm not uncomfortable?
What do I do so that I don't risk losing something I care about?
What do I do so that I don't look like a bozo?

We just explored our relationship to discomfort and tension. Now let's talk about our relationship to risk. For the sake of this conversation, let's be clear that *real* safety is very, very important. Absolutely. However, we also want to keep in mind that our primitive brains aren't so great at discerning between *real* safety and a threat to our discomfort or self-image.

This means that most of the time we're playing it far safer than we need to. And strangely enough, it's our desire to avoid screwing up that often screws things up. Here's an example of how I almost torched my marriage before it even got off the ground.

The Starbucks Shootout

Back in 2004, I was introduced to my wife, Alyson. At that time, she lived in Colorado and I lived in Florida. Because she's weird, she would only communicate with me via email, but after playing that game for a few months, she finally figured out how to use a phone, and one day we talked. And talked. And talked some more. We had an amazing conversation full of laughter and depth and more laughter.

I realized two things after I got off the phone: One, I had to meet this gal face to face, and two, I knew she was going to be in my life forever — either as a friend or maybe something more.

Now here's where I pulled the boss move, and I tell you this now because it won't be long until you witness my fall from grace. I got bold and called her back and said I was going to book a flight to Colorado so that I could take her out to dinner. And a week or so later, I got off the plane, met her at the restaurant, and we had a great first date. The energy was electric, the conversation effortless. We laughed and talked for hours, flowing between some of the most sacred elements of our spiritual beliefs right into grimy, profane gutter humor. This was my kind of gal. I was blown away. And as we made plans to spend more time together the following day, I heard a voice in my head saying, *Don't screw this up, man!*

Still with me? Good.

Cut to the next day, and we're driving around Boulder. It was freezing outside, but things between Alyson and me had gotten frosty as well. The exciting energy was gone. Any kind of sexual chemistry that was crackling the night before had vaporized, too. The conversation felt so stiff and awkward and shallow. I was a ball of tension wrapped up in self-consciousness. My thoughts were all over the place. *Don't screw this up, man! Don't do anything that'll ruin it!*

What I didn't realize at the time was that I had shifted gears. No longer bold and open to possibility, I was now playing defense. Instead of continuing in the mindset and flow that allowed me to have this opportunity in the first place, I was now struggling to make sure "I got this right." And this meant my head shot firmly up my ass — full of worries about how to act so that I didn't do anything that might rock the boat.

All of this taking things so seriously meant I wasn't having fun anymore. Instead, I was feeling trapped because I believed everything I said or did was a big deal that might screw up my opportunity. I felt drained because the conversation was sooooo boooooring. I definitely felt stressed because I believed the stakes were high, and even though we were physically in the same space together, I most certainly didn't feel connected to Alyson.

I didn't know what to do. I didn't even know what I wanted other than some relief from the pressure of trying to "not screw this up." I wasn't leading. I was hoping some magical dude-fairy would come along and tell me what to do.

Now, because I was so focused on myself and trying to "get it right," I didn't realize that all of this awkwardness was completely obvious to Alyson. I had no idea that instead of helping things get stronger, all of my efforts to play it safe were actually making things worse. And I was about to find out how much this was driving her nuts, too.

So we shuffled across the icy sidewalk and went into a Starbucks. The place was packed. She ordered some kind of foamy chai latte with cruelty-free dick sprinkles, and I was still over here trying to be Mr. Cool Guy.

The barista handed her the drink, and in the next few seconds my life changed forever.

Like an action hero in slow motion, Alyson swiftly pivoted to aim the lid of the cup right at my center mass. Simultaneously, her other hand swung upward and popped the bottom of the cup to send a giant stream of 2 percent soy vegan dick sprinkled chai latte foam all over me. Head to toe. Right there. In front of everybody.

For a few seconds I was in shock. Time stood still. Even that nauseating Starbucks music seemed to go silent. *What. The. Hell!?!* My brain struggled to recalibrate. First of all, that was an amazing shot. *Does she go to a gun range?* I looked up from my foam-covered body and saw Alyson's devilish smile. And that's when I dropped the "good guy" facade.

It. Was. On.

Like a panther — a soggy, chai-covered war panther — I panther-pounced through the crowd over to that counter where all of the condiments are, and unleashed a torrent of sugar packets down upon her. Without hesitation, she returned fire with another stream of foam accompanied by a squeal of delight. But before she could take cover she was pummeled by my Bruce Lee–inspired hellfire of coffee-stirrer-stick daggers. *WAAA-TA-AAAAAAAA!!!*

We laughed and yelled and ran around the tables full of serious people and their laptops. Stuff was flying everywhere. Mouths open, people stared at us like we were nuts. Collateral damage? I'm sure we lost a few good customers that day.

We ran out the door gasping, and in that moment of watching my breath turn to vapor I felt alive again. I felt like me again. I wasn't playing it safe anymore. I wasn't feeling stressed or drained or trapped anymore. I was *playing*. I was feeling free and alive and way more connected to Alyson.

And it wouldn't occur to me until later that Alyson's bold, risky action saved our relationship from a dismal, boring, day-date demise. Without that shootout in Starbucks, we wouldn't have gotten married, we wouldn't have our daughter, and we wouldn't have all of the joy that we share today.

Old Guys With a Stick Up Their Butt

The more we care about something — our money, our careers, our relationships, our self-image — the more serious we tend to become. We strive for more certainty, structure, direction, and order so that we'll feel safe and have a "competitive advantage" in the world. But here's the cruel paradox: the more we tend to care about something, the more we tend to become fixed and rigid. And the more rigid we get, the more vulnerable we become. Our efforts to protect — when out of balance — often make us a liability to ourselves. When we're constantly playing defense, we stop enjoying our lives, and we end up being one of those old farts who have a stick up their caboose about everything.

We do this by holding back, hiding out, and striving to "get it right" without ever challenging our fears. As our imagination conjures up threats of loss, we primitively react and jump on the brakes. When we blindly follow expectations and rules for how things "should be done," we kill our authority, creativity, and ingenuity. And no matter how good we are at "getting it right," this rigid, overly serious way of life leads us to feel trapped, drained, isolated, stressed out, or bored.

That's weak as fuck. So if we're committed to our strength, then let's expand our capacity to take risks. As we expand, we want to be smart. We want to be grounded while we *also* loosen up and challenge any beliefs that make us take things so seriously. And the easiest way to do this is to harness one of the powers we were all born with.

The Strong Choose to Play

Dr. Peter Gray[14] is a research professor of psychology at Boston College and the author of several books, including *Free to Learn*. Gray's research points to the decline of play in our younger people, how over the past sixty years we're playing less and spending more and more time in

---

14 Check out my interview with Dr. Peter Gray on The New Man Podcast.

"training" — in highly structured environments of expectations and control. As we've gotten more and more serious about getting into good schools and getting good jobs and keeping up with the Joneses, our young people spend more time "preparing" than playing. And Gray believes this is a strong contributor to the drastic rise of depression, anxiety, suicide, and narcissism in our younger generations.

But I don't think it's just the younger folks who are suffering. I believe the absence of a playful mindset in our adult lives is one of the main reasons why so many "successful" guys are getting fragile, too.

More and more we're being conditioned to believe that enjoyment, play, or pleasure are frivolous, a waste of time, a threat to our growth and progress. After all, we've got obligations to family and work. We've got bills to pay. We live in a world where we're constantly bombarded by headlines about potential diseases and harmful diets and failing markets and rising oceans and fish that'll crawl up your dickhole.[15] Our primitive brains have adapted to being in a constant state of freaking out. Even if we seemingly have it all, we tend to be way more fixated on protecting what we stand to lose.

So as we ramp up our efforts to prepare for all the possible outcomes, to give ourselves an advantage in the face of so much to worry about, we end up falling into that paradox. We put ourselves at a disadvantage because we forget how to be playful.

As part of his extensive research, Dr. Gray studies why mammals play, and basically he says play is in our DNA because it's essential to how we learn to deal with adversity. Play is at the heart of how we *grow* in the face of challenge. Play trains us to think on our feet and solve problems in the moment. This means being playful encourages us to experiment. It gives us a willingness to screw up from time to time. It opens up our imaginations to find powerful solutions to our problems. Being playful

---

15 It's called the Candirus and it lives in the Amazon river. Sweet dreams tonight, buddy.

guides us to find our own direction, build on what lights us up, and have the rewarding, meaningful experiences we most want to have.

Bottom line: being playful isn't about being silly or goofy. A playful mindset is at the heart of true leadership, innovation, and creativity. If we want to be strong, if we want to have an advantage when it comes to facing our challenges, then we want to pull the stick out of our asses and embrace our ability to find a playful approach to what we're creating.

But does being playful mean that we don't care anymore?

Want To Be At Your Best? Then Lighten Up

Our commitment to avoiding risk is rooted in fear. It's fear that has us believe we're more powerful when we pour on the pressure and urgency. We believe it's necessary to throw out our peace of mind in order to be powerful.

And it may *seem* powerful — especially if you're a little kid or a reality TV star — to get freaked out and upset and buy into the idea that our opportunities are scarce. It may *seem* powerful to throw a fit because, goddammit, they want to charge an extra thirty-five cents to use the parking meter. But when we're convinced that there's so much on the line and there's so much to lose, is that really where we're most creative and expansive and resourceful?

Years ago, I had a friend who played in a local hockey league out in Boulder. Apparently, he wasn't that great of a hockey player, but he did have one superpower — he could talk shit. The guy had a masters in psychology, and he would work ruthlessly to get inside the other team's mind and wear them down with his relentless taunting. Eventually, somebody on the other team would step into the trap. They'd get fed up, lose their temper, and end up in the penalty box, which would benefit the shit-talker's team. My friend knew that taking things too seriously was a liability, and he *played* them like a cheap fiddle.

Let's up the stakes a bit. Let's try something more serious. Let's talk about that time I almost sank my coaching business.

When I first started coaching, I was so serious about "getting it right" that it made me want to quit. In each session, my head was full of critical voices focusing on my performance. I imagined I was constantly on the verge of screwing something up. And because I was so afraid to get fired, I stayed in my shell and wouldn't take any risks.

With one foot on the gas and one foot on the brake, I would end each coaching session feeling exhausted and drained because I was hiding out — holding back my power. I was protecting my income. I was pleasing, doing whatever I could to avoid ruffling any feathers. I was trying to prove I was a "real" coach, and my clients were getting bored and drifting away.

So one day, I decided to quit being a coach. And I decided that if I was going to quit then I may as well be bold and play full out. With seemingly nothing to lose, I was free to coach in a way that was enlivening and fun. I wasn't trying to be reckless or burn anything down. I was just giving myself permission to stop taking things so seriously. I chose to follow my fun instead.

I prepared myself for the worst. I thought for sure I'd get fired or piss someone off. But it was the opposite. Because I was more relaxed, my clients were too. We started having fun, and the sessions got easier as we did more effective work. Instead of fixating on what could go wrong, I started taking risks that made a real difference. And this meant my clients got far more value. Imagine that.

So I made a commitment at that time that I still hold to this day, which is this: relax and find the fun. I remind myself before each call that if I'm coming from a place of service, then I'm willing to be fired in any given session. Sure, getting fired may suck, but playing it safe is a far bigger threat to my business in the long term.

Loosen Up Doesn't Mean Giving Up

Do me a favor and with your right hand make a really tight fist. I mean really tight. Make it so tight that your knuckles turn white. Keep it that way for a minute. Okay. Now make your other hand completely limp. Zero tension. Zero effort. Completely dead.

Our fear wants us to tighten up. It believes that when we're faced with a challenge, more is more, so we tend to end up with a tight, rigid, exhausted fist (it's pretty tired by now, isn't it?). And one of the reasons we have a hard time loosening up is because we think it means we have to *disengage*. We mistakenly believe that if we relax then we're going to go *allllllll* the way over to the other extreme where we're completely limp and useless, like your other hand.

But there's a whole middle ground between rigid, white-knuckling terror and those useless, flippy-flappy fingers. There's an entire range of motion where we can do millions of things with these very hands. By loosening up, we don't have to disengage. We empower ourselves to respond with greater flexibility, strength, and effectiveness.

Many times, we make excuses for using fear and pressure and self-criticism to motivate ourselves. We believe it gives us an edge. And to a degree it certainly can — until it makes us weak. Our job is to recognize when fear has us convinced we're on the verge of some "disaster," so that we can learn to challenge those fears, loosen up, and bring our best to the situation.

When we truly care about bringing strength to our challenges, then we want to question anything that makes us believe there's so much to fear.

Remember You're Not a Fragile Little Flower

When I was in college, I shared an apartment with two other guys. It was an absolute dump. It was hot. It smelled like stale beer, frozen pizza, and a petting zoo from hell. The toilet was growing its own beard. Yeah, that's right. A bacteria beard.

My bedroom was also the rehearsal space for my band, which meant I had to climb over a Neil Peart–sized drum kit just to get to bed every night. We were under constant threat of retribution for the pranks we pulled on others. There were times where we forgot how to do simple math, spent too much money on beer, and had to figure out how we were going to eat.

Looking back, you'd think we would talk about it like it was WWII Europe. But the truth is we had a blast. We laughed so much. We were always creating some kind of an adventure. We had very little money, and even though our apartment was infested with cockroaches, it never felt like a nightmare.

I started my first company when I was twenty-three, and one of the reasons I felt so confident back then was because I was already used to living with very little money. Knowing I'd be fine if things got tough financially gave me strength. It gave me confidence to take risks.

Now two-plus decades later, at least once a year, I find myself in a situation with my business where fear tries to convince me that this is the end.

Oh no. Oh no. Oh no. Is this it? Am I gonna end up selling plastic phone cases at a mall kiosk now? Are we gonna end up in some gross, stinky apartment?

Even though I've been facing and overcoming challenges in my business for more than twenty years, my fear still tries to convince me that I'm on the verge of "losing it all" from time to time. Even though I once lived in a cesspool and look back at it fondly, my fear still tries to convince me that giving up a few creature comforts would be *the end of the world*. Insert stick in butt. Goodbye, strength.

Now let's be clear. Really clear. I've lived with money and I've lived without much money and I very much prefer living with money. I'm very clear that I don't want to go back to living in a cesspool. The point I'm trying to make here is how quickly our "need" for comfort triggers our fear for *survival* and makes us less willing to take risks.

So let's not confuse a reduction in comfort with a reduction in safety. Let's not confuse a little challenge to our self-image with a risk to our mortality. Because when that happens, we forget just how much challenge and risk we can actually handle. Our amazing yet outdated brain forgets just how powerful we are. It wildly overestimates our challenges and grossly underestimates our power. And if we see ourselves as fragile — as someone who can't fall down and get back up, as someone who can't tolerate a bit of discomfort — then it's obvious that we'll overestimate our challenges and strive to avoid any risk.

So — what if we stopped believing that we're some fragile little flower? What if we stopped lying to ourselves and began to see ourselves in a more realistic way? What if we remembered that we literally had to learn how to fall and get back up *many times* in order to simply walk? What if we remembered how many times we've faced challenges and come out the other side just fine — or even stronger than before?

When we see ourselves as we are, we free up so much of our energy to do the stuff that matters. If we're going to get stronger, it's not going to be a product of running away from what scares us. If we're going to expand, it's going to be the product of challenging our fears and taking risks.

Challenge the Monsters Under Your Bed

A young child may run into his parents' room scared at night, *convinced* that there's a big bad monster under the bed. But do we, as adults, buy into the fantasy? No. The *experience* of fear is real. But we know the actual threat is not.

Well, could it be possible that we've grown into adult bodies but still imagine big bad monsters in our work, relationships, and personal lives? Could it be possible that we're still finding ways to live in fear, based solely on a fantasy in our head? Yes. Bet on it.

When I'm working with coaching clients who are convinced that there's a gigantic, scary monster in their lives, we don't brainstorm strategies for running away. We consciously choose to show up as a mature adult instead of a scared, wounded child. We figuratively grab a flashlight and go take a look.

Let's see if there's really a monster under the bed.

I may ask a client who's dealing with a challenge with his business partner…

"Okay, you're frustrated with how things are going. So, what do you want?"

"Well, I want to make a change to our operating agreement, but, uh, that's where I get stuck."

"What's the story, what's the assumption that you have? It doesn't have to make sense. We just want to get your concerns out in front of us so that we can see them."

"Okay. I'm worried that my partner's going to think I'm being greedy. I'm scared he's going to think I'm trying to push him out."

"And is that the case? Is that true?"

"No. Not at all."

"Okay. So what are you concerned will happen if he believed that you were greedy and trying to push him out?"

"Um. I'm worried that he'll get upset. I'm not really sure exactly, but it wouldn't be good. Yelling? Lawyers? Who knows?"

"Got it. So the big scary idea is that just bringing up the idea of a change could eventually send everything down the toilet. Is that right?"

"Yeah. Kill the business. Kill our friendship. No more family vacations together, you know?"

"Okay. And how long have you had this concern? How long have you been wanting to address this with him?"

"Oh gosh. At least two years. I knew we had a problem with this arrangement a long time ago."

"And you're not speaking up because you assume that he'll think you're being greedy. That he'll get upset and then sue you and then your families couldn't hang out anymore?"

"Jeez. I haven't thought of it like that, but yeah. I was just hoping something would come along and kind of take care of it."

"Like magic. Okay, so as we shine a light on your concerns, does what you want still sound so risky?"

"Not really. As I talk about it, I can see that our partnership is solid. We can talk about this stuff. And even if he got upset, it's not like everything would come crashing down immediately. We can work it out. I've just been avoiding it."

"Makes sense. So what if it wasn't so bad and so scary? What if this could open up the possibility for greater expansion for both of you? Who knows? Maybe he's sitting on some concerns as well. What would it look like if you focused on the possibilities instead of what may get lost?

Could this be a more creative or even playful opportunity?"

"Huh. That's interesting. I haven't even considered that. Yeah. You know, it would be cool if he and I just went for a hike and gave ourselves a chance to talk about what we both want and where we want to go. That's how we got the idea for this business — on a hike."

"I like that. So instead of sinking the ship, this could be a more expansive, co-creative opportunity.'"

"It could be."

"And could the operating agreement be a part of that conversation?"

"Absolutely."

"And so what do you want to do?"

"I'm going to ping him and see if he'd join me for a hike where we could zoom out and talk about all of this stuff."

"You've waited two years already. Is there a reason why you should wait any longer? Could you send the invitation right now?"

"Ooof. Ha. Yeah, I guess I could."

"Great. Go ahead and send him that text. I'll wait."

It's amazing how often we — grown-ass men — are making our lives smaller because we're unwilling to take some risks. And you know what happens most of the time when we do choose to step into our fears? *Nothing*. In fact, usually as soon as we even name our big, bad, terrible nightmare scenario, we can immediately see that it's just a fantasy. When we're willing to take the time to simply shine a light on the stories we're telling ours elves, we can see how we're being held hostage by an unconscious, irrational fear.

Let's give it a try right now. *Let's see.*

Put Your Fears in Perspective

Grab your journal or whatever you like to write with. And then, let's get curious about your frustration — whatever's draining you, whatever has you feeling trapped, whatever is zapping your peace of mind.

Take a few minutes to focus on this particular area of your life and write at least ten answers to this sentence stem:

I'm frustrated (or drained or trapped or stressed or bored) because

1. _____.
2. _____.
3. _____.
4. _____.
5. _____.
6. _____.
7. _____.
8. _____.
9. _____.
10. _____.

No need to edit or even make any rational sense. No need to judge it either. Just give yourself permission to write down whatever crazy answers come to you.

And now, let's add a new sentence:

I can't do anything about this because

1. _____.
2. _____.
3. _____.
4. _____.
5. _____.
6. _____.
7. _____.
8. _____.
9. _____.
10. _____.

Again, write down as many answers as you can. And again, no need to judge or edit or worry about what comes out. Just get it out.

Next, we want to take a look at those answers and go a bit deeper.

If I actually tried to do any of this stuff to make a positive change then _____ would happen and then _____ would happen and then _____ would happen.

And, you guessed it, just write it all out unfiltered. Keep unraveling these imagined consequences until you reach the absolute, most awful, terrible scenario possible. This is the big, scary monster under the bed.

Now take a look at your answers. Read through them. How much of this is true? How much of this is an assumption? How much of this is highly unlikely?

In order for that worst-case scenario to occur, how many other things would have to completely fall apart first? I know that when I talk to guys who are fearful about losing their business or job, they seem to believe that within minutes of walking out the door, they would be in an alley trying to find a dishwasher box to sleep in. They don't see how so many other crappy events would have to occur before the absolute worst scenario became a reality. They forget their power. They forget that they would be able to take action and find ways to turn things around well before that occurred.

Bottom line: this little exercise can be a step in the direction of empowerment. It can help us see that things aren't as dreadful as we may have imagined. And it can help us see that our risks are much smaller than our young, fearful brains would have us believe.

Now, let's get something clear — I want to kill this false idea that just because we can see that our problems are no big deal, we won't feel scared from time to time. That's insane. We are still going to experience our fear on a regular basis. We will still freak out from time to time, *and* we can learn to give ourselves space to have that freak-out. We are highly complex, emotional creatures, and we're going to have our emotional reactions. It happens, but we don't have to act or make choices *from* that mindset. Instead of bottling it up and giving ourselves emotional constipation, we can learn to simply let that energy move through us and then pivot back into our adult selves. We can take action from a more grounded, mature perspective.

Okay. I'm scared. I'm going to do some breathing. I'm going to go for a walk. I'm going to talk to a friend. And then I'm going to figure out how to respond powerfully.

Let's look at another way to minimize our risks.

Game Over — Scarcity and the Myth of Finality

Imagine you're a kid playing a video game in the arcade. You're about to hit your high score, but you only have *one* life left.

This is it. I've only got one shot.

Hello, pressure. Hello, fear. And when we're in this state of mind, how do we play? When our opportunities feel limited, do we play full out? Or do we hold back, contract, and get smaller?

This is it. I can't screw this up.

Even though the game only cost a quarter (back then), we may have lost sight of the fact that we were *playing a game*. Today, while we may no longer be scrounging around in sofa cushions looking for quarters to play an arcade game, many of us are approaching our lives with this same mentality. We really believe so much in our lives is final.

This product launch has got to work. Otherwise, it's game over.
I've only got a certain amount of money for a runway to build this business. Otherwise, it's game over.
If this relationship doesn't work out, then that's it. It's game over.

The Myth of Finality is one of our favorite ways to freak ourselves out. When we believe that we only have one shot, we approach the most important areas of our lives in a rigid and narrow mindset. We don't take chances. We don't experiment. And we certainly don't have any fun.

Here's why — at the root of this Myth of Finality is our belief that what we ultimately want is the *outcome*, the *result*. When we're stuck in this myth, it means we've forgotten that we're playing for the *experiences* of freedom, aliveness, love, and peace. And when we understand that the outcomes and results are only pathways to the experiences we most want, we can start to identify other pathways. In other words, when we drop our fixation on outcomes and pathways, we have more than one shot. We have many opportunities between the time we're born and the day that we die to experience the freedom, aliveness, love, and peace that we want.

If I don't get this promotion, then I'll figure it out. It's not the end for me.
If I run out of runway money and don't launch this business as planned, then I'll figure it out. It's not the end for me.
If this relationship ends, it'll suck, but I'll figure it out. It's not the end for me.

Sure, it may suck to take a loss when the outcomes we want go south, but that doesn't have to block our ability to experience freedom, aliveness, love, and peace *forever*. If we're willing to remember how powerful we are, if we're willing to focus on the experiences that truly matter, then we're able to put risk in perspective.

This is what allows us to loosen up. This is what allows us to be more creative and agile. And this is what opens us up to play.

You Can Fucking Do That?

Growing up in the armpit of pre-internet Florida surrounded by swamps and orange groves, opportunities for life looked pretty uninspiring to say the least. As a kid finishing up the eleventh grade, I had very little sense of what life could be like after school. I imagined that, like so many of the grownups I knew, my high school days were probably going to be my glory days. *Oooof.*

Fortunately, my Dad took me down to Miami to spend a few days with a guy who shattered my expectations about how one could live and work.

This was a guy who had his own creative agency, designed his schedule so he could surf a bunch, and even lined up his clients' photoshoots in places with great surf. Instead of being stuck in a senseless grind, this guy seemingly designed his work around the lifestyle he wanted. He seemed to break all the rules for what *work* was supposed to be.

And as a young — very, very, very — innocent kid who believed he was facing decades of 9-to-5 monotony and drudgery, I had one thing to say…

You can fucking do that?

Apparently, yes. Yes, you can. Inspired by this guy's example, I was determined to create my own version. I graduated from college a few years later and started my own company with the bold, crazy, risky intention of making a living in a way that supported the lifestyle I wanted. I built a business that empowered me to have fun — make my own records, surf, travel, whatever. And it certainly wasn't easy. There was a lot of that hard work, and risky, bold stuff going on.

Years later, I was at a weird gathering for artists and art-types and noticed this older guy standing around, chewing on a cigar. I walked up to him and struck up a conversation.

"So, uh, what kind of art do you do?"

"You could say I'm into mixed media."

"Oh, okay. And what kind of materials do you use?"

"I do collage. I find ways to put businesses together."

Boom. Mind blown.

You can fucking do that?

Yeah, apparently you can. Here was a guy who had an artistic approach to life, but instead of farting around with paints and clays and crap he found in a junkyard, he created artful ways to combine companies and products and offerings. And while it looked like "doing business" from the outside, he was very clear that it was art. It was *play*.

I've met quite a few of these inspiring folks over the years, and I always have the same response when I see how they approach their lives with a playful mindset. *You can fucking do that?* These are the folks who are able to clarify what they want, be bold enough to actually own it, and then do the work to make it happen. They challenge their fears and the voices that say, "That's not how you're supposed to do it" and they take some risks in service of what feels enlivening and fun for themselves. They don't wait around for a winning lottery ticket. They don't wait around for permission from god-knows-who. Instead of getting mired in someone else's game, they have the guts and discipline to play their own.

Let's break this process down so we can find ways to play our own game, too.

Challenge the Rules and Expectations

Whether we're talking about our personal growth, our fitness, our business development, our relationships, or whatever — like we did earlier, we want to look at the places in our life where we feel trapped or drained or isolated or stressed out. These are the doorways to greater expansion. We want to get curious and listen to the message that our pain in the ass is trying to deliver.

And let's consider that one of the reasons this particular area feels draining is because we have a belief, an expectation, a rule that's been screwed into our skulls.

I have to do it this way. This is just how it's done.[16]

This can cover everything from how we choose to exercise to how we create prospects for our business to how we have sex with our partner to how we spend time with our family. We settle for the draining, boring, or stressful option because our parents or friends or some asshat in a book told us that "this is how you're supposed to do it."

I have to wake up super early every day. That's what successful people do.
Staying fit has to be super intense and grinding. That's what makes it a good workout.
Creating a new business is a hustle. You have to be driven by fear and scarcity or you'll lose your edge to the competition.
Sex with your spouse just gets boring. Look around. It's inevitable. Talk about it with her? Are you crazy?

And so we just go along with it. We play that game because, chances are, we've been conditioned to follow the rules, color within the lines, and meet expectations. But if we're feeling bored or drained or trapped by these patterns, what might be possible when we're willing to challenge them? Is it really true that this is the way things *have to* be done? Is it really true that these "rules" can't be broken? Who the heck decided these were the rules?

Here's where we build on the work we did earlier. Here's where we tap into our inner authority. Here's where we step into our power.

These rules and ideas may have worked for that person, but what works for me? What has me feel stronger and more expansive?

Again, just because we don't see any other options on the menu doesn't

---

[16] If you find yourself saying "I have to..." often, chances are you're operating from a victim mentality. Check out the Drama Triangle video I mentioned earlier.

mean there aren't other options available. And to find the most energizing, expansive option we want we can learn to ask ourselves one simple question…

What Would Make This Fun?

Yeah. What *would* make this fun? If we're getting in shape or building our business or reigniting the flame in our marriage, who says it has to be a slog? What would make it energizing? What would make it playful?

We don't have to let fear convince us that the situation is too risky. We don't have to take things too seriously. We don't have to be rigid. We don't have to make ourselves weaker in order to "succeed." We can challenge the idea that there's so much at stake. We can loosen up without giving up. We can step into a playful mindset and access our greatest creativity and resilience. And to do this, we follow our fun.

Follow the Fun

Pick an area of your life where you feel some friction. Where are things feeling like a grind? Where are things feeling boring? What are you wanting to escape?

Grab something to write on, and jot down the choices — the actions you take every day or week to create a specific outcome. The meetings or the drive or the networking gatherings or whatever you believe you *have to* do. Write them down.

And then let's identify the rules and expectations that govern those choices.

In order to _____,

I have to _____.

Fill in those blanks as much as possible. Connect the dots between the actions you take and the outcomes you want. And then zoom out. These statements are the rules or expectations that you're following.

For instance…

In order to have new prospects coming in, I have to go to at least three crappy networking events per week.

In order to stay in shape, I have to wake up at 5 a.m. to get to the gym every day.

In order to keep my wife happy, I have to take her to Long John Silver's every Thursday night.

Chances are, you still want those outcomes — the new prospects, staying in shape, a strong connection with your wife — but maybe you're sick of the specific *processes*. So let's challenge the idea that these rules are fixed in stone.

Is it really true that in order to have ABC, I have to also do XYZ? Is this really the only way?

Now, considering other possibilities is where we can expect to feel our fear. Considering other options may feel a little risky. Breaking from the conventional norm can have us believe there are all kinds of monsters under the bed.

But if I make a change, then I might go broke! I might backslide into obesity! I might end up ruining my marriage!

Big, scary monsters, indeed. But we can challenge those, too. *What if it wasn't true that this terrible thing would happen if we tried a different strategy? What if we found something that worked even better?*

And as we begin to loosen up a bit, we can invite our creativity into the conversation. *We could warm up that muscle and begin to ask, What would make this fun?*

Instead of wishing for an escape from work, what would be a fun way to create more prospects? Instead of hoping for a magic pill, what would be a fun way to stay active and fit? Instead of fantasizing about a different partner, what would be a fun, fresh way to connect with your existing partner?

I want to keep new prospects coming in. What would make it fun? Spending more time with folks that are into the same things I'm into would be cool. I'm going to join the local surf club this Tuesday, and see if I can make some connections there.

I want to be fit, but I hate waking up early just to move heavy stuff around a stinky gym. What would make it fun? That crazy Fight Club workout group that meets in the park sounds interesting. Kinda scary, but also really fun. I'm going to try that out tomorrow.

I want to keep things solid with my wife, but we're really in a rut. What would make it fun? This week I'm going to break out of our pattern and surprise her with a scavenger hunt date where we have to drive around the city to find clues for our next vacation.

For your specific situation, give yourself permission to write down as many fun, outlandish ideas as you can imagine. Don't worry about what is doable just yet. We simply want to rebuild this mental ability to find fun, and it'll take some work if you've been expecting the sky to fall at any moment.

Write down at least twenty ideas that would be fun, and then pick one to try. Make an agreement with yourself about when you'll follow through, and then go do it. Keep going. Keep building this muscle and you'll learn — through experience — how being playful can help you break out of the ruts that drain you.

When to Knock the Hustle

When it comes to my clients who own their own business, the tendency to "hustle" is a pandemic. In order to be "successful" they constantly compare themselves to idealized, photoshopped versions of other business owners and grind themselves to a pulp trying to keep up with a fantasy. And they often find, in the process, that what seemingly works for others is a real drag for them. So, instead of letting fear drive them to blindly mimic what others are doing, we learn to follow our fun. We learn to lead and reveal what is most effective for them as individuals.

If it drains me to be on social media, then who says I have to do it that way? What's a more fun way to connect with and serve the people I want to work with?

If it drains me to roll out a new offering like the other guys, then who says I have to do it that way? What's a more fun way to bring my product to market?

This is *real* leadership. It's a willingness to play to what strengthens us instead of following the scarcity mentality of the herd. We've seen how companies[17] that play to their strengths can disrupt an entire industry. And when these leaders arrive on the scene, it leaves the rest of us wondering…

You can fucking do that?

Yes. Yes you can, if you're willing to drop the victim mentality and choose empowered responses. Yes you can, if you're willing to drop the wounded

---

[17] For example, companies like Amazon, Airbnb, and Tesla all started out as scrappy underdogs that played their own game and revolutionized their respective industries.

belief that we need to earn our good fortune through misery and complexity. Yes you can, if you're willing to be bold and take risks. Yes you can, if you can find a way to be playful and do what needs to be done with discipline and consistency.

When Safety is an Illusion

It *seems* safer to follow the herd, to follow the rules and expectations. It *seems* safer to walk the path most traveled. It *seems* safer to just go with the flow. But we can't allow ourselves to fall asleep at the wheel. By paying attention to where we feel trapped, drained, isolated, or overwhelmed, we can learn to recognize when "getting it right" is killing our strength — whether we're building a business or taking a date to Starbucks. We can recognize our ability to challenge our monsters under the bed, take risks, and follow our fun instead.

If we truly care about our safety and success, then it's far more sustainable to choose a path that builds our fire as we go instead of depriving ourselves, hoping for an escape that may never come. We don't need to withhold play from our lives like some circus animal waiting for a treat after he jumps through a flaming hoop. We can learn to incorporate playfulness into everything we do.

Which means we have one more area to address when it comes to building strength. We've been learning that we can be bold to take on discomfort, and we can be playful to take on risk. Now, let's talk about how we can address one more commitment.

CHAPTER 7:

Get Over Yourself — Live as if There's Nothing to Prove and Play for Something Bigger

Okay. Here we go.

We've expanded some ways to deal with our primitive, limiting efforts to avoid discomfort and risk. Now it's time to address the last, but most powerful of our modern challenges — anything that threatens our self-image.

Earlier, we discussed how many of us believe freedom is the ability to take any road we want, to explore all that life has to offer. We imagine that money and status will free us from the constraints of life and open all the doors to everything we want — the luxuries, the travel, the sex, the adoration, whatever. And while having the flexibility to explore lots of options may be amazing, I'm not convinced it points to the freedom we really want.

I found a Bruce Lee quote that says…

"Freedom discovers the man the moment he loses concern over what impression he is making or about to make."

Now we're getting closer. This points to freedom as a state of being, a way of living free from concerns and burdens and worries. And again, many of us believe we'll achieve this state of being once we've accomplished our goals, once we've defended our status, and once we've finally proven that we're enough.

But what if the opposite were true? Instead of striving for some magical finish line of "enough," what if this experience of freedom emerges when we let go of the striving and the defending and the proving altogether? What if our peace of mind emerges when we relax our need to defend ourselves against the threatening possibility that we're just not that big of a deal?

Because no matter what we say or do or believe — we are never going to be a big deal.

Let's put things into perspective.

You're Not a Big Deal

When we think of big — and I mean really big — we usually think of the sun. It's massive, right? In fact, you could fit 1.3 *million* Earths inside of the sun. Let that sink in.

But according to astronomer and scientist Michelle Thaler, if you were to shrink the sun down to the size of the dot in this letter "i" right here on the page — that tiny-ass little dot — if you made the sun that big, then the relative size of our galaxy, the Milky Way, would be the size of the Earth. Take a minute to visualize that.

But let's not stop there. A while back, astronomers found a tiny section of the night sky that appeared to be empty. And "tiny" means the size of the head of a pin if you held it out at arm's length. If you were to hold that tiny pinhead up to the sky, then that little, tiny portion of the sky appeared to be completely void of celestial light. So they focused the Hubble Telescope up there, and let it absorb light for ten days.

And in that tiny, tiny dark part of the night sky which looked completely empty, they ended up discovering *3,000 galaxies.*

Holy. Shit.

So what does this all mean? You, me, all of us — our daily crises and dramas and getting pissed off because the barista forgot to put 3.5 percent soy vegan dick sprinkles in our lattes — when we start to imagine this massive universal perspective, we start to see that no matter what we are thinking or doing, it's really just not that big of a deal. And it never will be.

Does that mean we should just give up? That life is pointless? How can we possibly live our lives if we're so infinitely small?

Maybe you feel a little deflated right now. I get it. But consider this — the part of you that feels a little deflated is probably just the part of you that *believes* it needs to be important or outstanding or significant. Consider this possibility: what if that's not all of who we are? What if we are more than just our need to be important or appreciated or the center of attention?

Being Self-Absorbed is a Luxury

When I'm working with a coaching client, most of the time the thing that's holding him back from creating what he truly wants isn't a lack of information or even a lack of resources. It's just fear — what many point to as a fear of failure.

Now, when we say we have a fear of failure, it's highly unlikely that we're going to have to sell a kidney in order to keep a roof over our heads. Think about it. How often are those of us in our privileged, cushy culture ever threatened on a mortal, physical level? Very, very, very rarely. And that's amazing. Because that's not true for most of the people on this planet. Being self-absorbed is a luxury.

That said, instances of anxiety and depression in our culture are continuing to climb. But it's not because our survival is at stake. It's largely because we've convinced ourselves that who we are and what we're doing is *such a big deal*. And this has us over-prioritize and over-emphasize our need to "get it right," to fit in, to be important and outstanding.

So, from this universal perspective, I invite you to consider just how liberating this realization can be. You see, if we don't need to attach so much importance to ourselves, if we don't need to be so wound up about the seemingly small stuff, then that frees us up to play *big*.

It's a paradox — to play full out without being attached to the outcome. It's way easier said than done. And I'm not going to act like I'm somehow enlightened and able to do this all the time.

But what if we could begin to consider that a threat to our self-image or ego wasn't really a threat? What if the fears we have about who we think we are and how we should look and how we should act and what others may think are overrated?

There were times in our past when we, as humans, believed things that seemed undeniable. We believed that throwing virgins off a cliff would make it rain. We believed that sending money to a preacher in Oklahoma would cure our bunions. And we believed that the Earth was flat (some are still holding fast to this idea). What if some of the stories we're telling ourselves today are just as wacky?

In many ways, the fears tied to our self-image are more dreams than reality. Like dreams, they only exist in our minds. And perhaps with practice, we'll be able to "wake up" and remember that, on a deep, essential level, we're more than our need to be a big deal.

When we practice putting things into perspective, instead of getting all precious and fragile, instead of holding back or avoiding or hiding out, we can lean in and create what we truly want in the short time that we have to be alive. We don't have to attach our well-being to how well we measure up to others or how well we meet the expectations of others. We can relax our need to protect and please and prove. We can let go of fixating on the outcomes, and instead focus on the *experiences* of freedom, aliveness, love, and peace that we most want. We can open ourselves up to greater meaning and depth.

So with that said, let's see if we can dismantle some of the ways we take ourselves too seriously.

The Fear of Mediocrity

When we tap into our ambition, we find our deep desire to win, to be better than we were yesterday, to be better than the rest. For some of us it may go a step further — we can't just be better, we have to be *the best*. The best in our family, the best in our class, the best in our office, the best in our industry, the best in our little world — you get the picture. Let's appreciate how this kind of drive has made our lives better in terms of technology, sports, and business.

But like anything in life, this ambition can get out of balance.

When I interviewed Dr. Michael Gervais, who is a high-performance psychologist for the Seattle Seahawks and Fortune 100 companies, he agreed. He said, "Most people that I spend time with are the tip of the arrow, half percenters of the world. They're changing industry, changing their sport, and most of them are driven underneath by anxiety. There's a dark side to trying to become your best or be the best."

And that's because this drive is often rooted in fear — the fear that someone might reveal the truth that we're just not that great. We're just not that special. Deep down, so many of us are using our accomplishments, income, social connections, job title, and anything else we can imagine to constantly defend ourselves. We're constantly managing and controlling and proving and bunkering against the possibility that some voice will say…

Someone else went farther than you. Someone else accomplished more than you. Someone else is better than you. You're not enough. And, therefore, you're not wanted.

Ouch.

This is why, for many of us, losing can mean we're a loser. Being average, being "mediocre," being "in the middle" instead of up there on the podium *feels* like a form of death to our precious, primitive self-image.

For others, it's our need to stand out, to be special, to be unique that is our way of proving that we're *somebody*. Because being another face in the crowd, being boring, or being invisible means we're a nobody. And for some, being a nobody *feels* like a form of death.

When we get stuck in this kind of mindset, we give up our inner authority. Which means we look outside of ourselves for direction and validation. Like runners in a sprint, we can't seem to go through life without looking side to side, without comparing ourselves to "the competition" in order to assess our self-worth. And if we're not careful, the fun and play that naturally comes from competition can turn into a never-ending pissing match to prove that we're not a loser. If we're not careful, we may live in a world of urgency and pressure to *always* be winning, to *always* be progressing, to *always* be proving, regardless of whether it makes us stronger or not.

Instead of aligning our lives with what has us feel more expansive, we tolerate chronic pressure to live up to some ideal of perfection that we have for ourselves. We block our ability to simply enjoy our life because, deep down, we don't believe we deserve our happiness. Deep down, we believe we have to suffer for it. We have to *earn it*.

Yuck.

So when I interviewed Barry Michels, a renowned psychotherapist and author who works with celebrities and high performers, he had some ideas for how we can reframe this desire to be on top.

He said that when we're motivated by extrinsic or *external* comparisons, we set ourselves up for constant disappointment. That's because there's always going to be someone who makes more, does it better, does it faster, gets more attention, etc. Which means winning may certainly be rewarding for a moment, but ultimately it's a losing game *if* we attach our sense of well-being to these types of outcomes.

When we strive to be the best, when we strive to *get* attention and validation and self-worth through wins, income, and rankings, it puts our peace of mind on a rollercoaster. We get weaker when we're dependent upon how we did compared to someone else or something outside of our control. Our experience of well-being goes up, down, up, down, up, down.[18]

But when get over ourselves and relax our need to get approval from the world, then we reclaim our power. We can tap into our *intrinsic* motivation — our inner authority. We can learn to play our own game and bring our best to whatever we're doing simply because the process itself strengthens us. We're no longer defined by our results. We're no longer exhausted by turning everything into a pissing match. The roller coaster smooths itself out. And if the awards and adoration show up, well then, that's just the cherry on top.

Bottom line: We get stronger when we relax our attachment to expectations, comparisons, and achievements, and instead choose to focus more on the activities and relationships and processes that have us feel more

---

[18] If you want to hear more about how Barry Michels works with big personalities and their drive to be "the best" check out my interview with him on The New Man Podcast.

expansive. Striving to be the best is a trap, but bringing our best to what we do allows us to live with greater freedom and possibility. Especially if we're willing to get over how we may appear to others.

But you may be thinking, *I'm not one of those guys seeking the spotlight or striving to be on some podium. I'm not self-absorbed.*

Don't be so sure.

Stop Being a Dick

It may seem easy to imagine that we're talking solely to the ones who want to stand out or be different from the rest of the herd. But what if our desire to fit in and please others is just another way that we protect our self-image? What if this desire to blend in with the crowd is what limits our opportunities?

Daniel Priestley[19] has had success as an entrepreneur with businesses all around the world. He's written some groundbreaking books on how to build companies, and we spent some time coaching together.

Contrary to those seeking the podium or spotlight, many of us are quite fearful of looking like the arrogant, showboating douche who distorts his importance and significance. So instead we go to the other extreme and try to appear *humble* — we withdraw, we hide out, we fade into the background. Instead of *inflating* how we appear, we end up *deflating* how we appear.

Priestley points out that these are both egoic distortions of the truth. They're both two sides of the same coin in which we're fixated on how we appear to ourselves and others. Ultimately, they're both ways that we limit our ability to experience greater freedom, aliveness, love, and peace because we're so attached to what others may think of us.

---

19 Check out my interview with Daniel Priestley, author of *Key Person of Influence* and *Oversubscribed* on The New Man.

But here's the really frustrating part about striving to be "humble" — when we distort and minimize the way that we see ourselves, we minimize our power and close the doors to opportunities. When we see ourselves as small, we only see opportunities that are small. And if an amazing opportunity does knock on our door, we push it away and settle for much, much less because we've bought into this bullshit, small image of ourselves.

That's not for me. I'm not one of those guys. I don't deserve that.

Priestley says that this egoic desire to appear smaller than we actually are ends up hurting others as well. After all, if we have a product or service or offering that will actually help the world, then why would we want to make it harder for folks to benefit from it? If we have the ability to help folks create positive changes in their lives, relationships, or businesses, then how are we benefiting others when we play this goofy game of "humility"?

Aww, shucks. What do I know? I'm nothing special. Who am I to think I can help somebody else?

Sadly, I've heard this kind of stuff spew out of the mouths of folks who have decades and thousands of hours of experience and a long list of amazing outcomes that they've helped others create. And yet they're still carrying around this outdated image of themselves. *Who am I to think I can help other people?*

And when you think about it long enough, it's easy to see how this self-absorbed defense is kind of a dick move. If we have a skill or offering that can really help people, and we're hiding out, then I've got one thing to say…

Stop being a dick.

Seriously. Let's stop making it about us and just own the truth that we are capable of making a difference.

If I've got a clogged pipe and I call a plumber, I don't want my plumber to have to wrestle with his self-image issues just so he can show up and snake my shitter. I just want him to get to my house and snake my shitter. Making it about him just gets in the way. It impedes his ability to help me and my family and that atrocity in my bathroom.

So — what if we didn't *need* to inflate our self-image in order to prove that we were important? What if we didn't *need* to deflate who we are in order to prove that we belonged?

In other words — what if there was nothing to prove?

What If There Was Nothing to Prove?

So many of us are waiting until we've proven that we are powerful or worthy or *enough* before we give ourselves permission to live the way we truly want to live. Well, just for a second, let's imagine that we're already there. Let's imagine that we've accomplished everything we set out to accomplish, that we've crossed that magical finish line. Let's imagine that we're finally *free* — there's nothing left to defend or justify to anything or anyone anywhere.

Yeah. How does that feel? Nice, huh?

Because here's the deal: if we're willing to take on a little discomfort, a little risk, and get over ourselves, then we can start to live that way today. Right now. We're not powerless. It's simply a choice.

Let's get more specific…

How would we show up in the world if we didn't *always* need to appear right or smart or legit or strong or the best or important or unique? How would we show up in the world if we didn't *always* need to be recognized or accepted or helpful or in control? How would we show up in the world if we didn't *always* need to rescue others or point out injustice or defend someone else?

What if we didn't *need* to scale or constantly grow just for the sake of growing? What if we didn't *need* more, more, and more of anything? Or, what if we didn't *need* to keep a foot on the brake because we were afraid of being too big? What if we didn't *need* to hide our strengths and talents and gifts from the world because we're afraid of negative attention?

Think of all the draining crap we choose to tolerate every day — the high cost of living, the debt for status symbols, the schmucks, the isolation, the refusal to ask for help, the need to make things hard or complex. How much of this crap would we continue to choose if there was no longer anything to prove?

I no longer tolerate these schmucks. I no longer have to prove that I'm powerful.

I no longer choose to live in this crowded city just to struggle in this draining career. I no longer have to prove that I'm legit.

I no longer refuse to see a therapist with my wife. I no longer have to prove that I always have my shit together.

Our need to prove often comes from the very powerful influence of others — parents, in-laws, teachers, friends, co-workers, Beyoncé. So if you've lived your entire life trying to prove to a parent or some group of people that you're enough, then ask yourself…

How would I live if this person (or these people) had never been born? How much of this song-and-dance and jumping through hoops and self-flagellation would I continue to tolerate?

These questions are just a start, but they're a way for us to see a life beyond the debilitating strategies most of us rely on for navigating the world. As a practice, asking ourselves these questions day in and day out can help us get a glimpse of a much more aligned way to live. And we'll know we're on the right track when we hear another voice pipe up and ask…

You can fucking do that?

Yes. Yes you can. It takes practice. It requires us to be bold. It requires us to be playful. So every day, take some time to get curious about the places in your life where you feel trapped or drained or isolated or stressed or bored, and then play with these questions. Explore what could be possible for you if there was no longer anything to defend or justify or prove.

We can learn through experimentation that the experiences we most want — freedom, aliveness, love, and peace — often arise when we simply relax and create space for them. We'll find that they're not a product of hiding out or blending in or striving or chasing or cramming more, more, more into our lives. In fact it's usually the opposite. We become stronger and more expansive when we drop the urgency, drop the fear of missing out, and let go of our need to defend our precious self-image — to do anything to prove that we're acceptable or special or worthy.

Life is Too Serious to Be Taken Seriously

If we believe we don't deserve our good fortune, if all we see are faults and injustices and imbalances, then we'll always find reasons to keep our joy out of reach. Many times this allergy to happiness is cultural. It's a product of growing up around people who couldn't allow themselves to be happy, so they sure as shit weren't going to let us be happy either.

But if we're willing to take responsibility for our life experience, then we can start to see through our limiting programming. We can recognize the choices we make to feed our addiction to misery and drama and pain. We can see that conflict is what our egos use to prove that we matter, that we *exist*. We can see that our self-criticism is just another way for us to fixate on ourselves and our need for self-importance because, *Oh my god, everything is so important!*

No matter what we may believe, being important is not the purpose of our lives. And this is why we need a sense of humor. It's not always easy, but life's a lot more fun when we get over ourselves. And the key to getting over ourselves is to learn how to *laugh* at ourselves. As the mysterious and controversial spiritual guru Sri Sri Sri Spankneesh Ji[20] once said in his thick, eastern Indian accent:

"Listen to me. We cannot take this life so seriously, and I mean that seriously. Life is too serious to be taken seriously."

Humor and laughter are essential to our ability to lighten up, forgive ourselves when we screw up, and remember that it's really not that big of a deal.

Ha! There I go again. Taking myself so seriously. Oh, well. Now how do I want to respond? What would have me feel stronger and more expansive?

Only the Dead Survive

When I coached with Phil Stutz[21] (who has spent decades forging a unique set of "tools" to overcome fear, as well as co-authoring *The Tools* and *Coming Alive*), he taught a powerful, simple lesson, which is this…

Only the dead survive.

Which means the key to *living* fully is another paradox. Let me explain.

---

20 You can check out my interview with this dubiously "enlightened" master on The New Man.

21 Here's another reminder to check out my interviews with Phil Stutz and Barry Michels. And do yourself a favor and read their books *The Tools* and *Coming Alive*.

When we're willing to do the things that *feel* like death to us — most specifically to our self-image and how we "need" to be seen — then we can be reborn when life inevitably hands us a loss. We find our strength when we're willing to steer right into the discomfort and risk and possibility of humiliation that *feels* like death. And it's this willingness to "die" — to get over ourselves — that allows us to be reborn to new opportunities again and again, long before our hearts stop beating.

Sounds simple enough, but if you've got a sizable ego like me, then you know this stuff is easier said than done. It would be a mistake to think that our highly sensitive — and highly defended — egos are just going to surrender without a fight. So let's go over a few practices that will help us keep our big heads in check.

We're More Powerful When We Give Up Hope

Likes. Attention. Approval. Appreciation. Recognition. Adoration. Being Desired.

Whether we want to admit it or not, so many of us imagine we're constantly being watched, judged, and assessed by *them* — whoever *they* may be. We do our thing — we make money or accomplish some big goal or step on the scale — and then ask, *How did I do? Was it good enough?* And from this mindset, we're making our work and relationships and sex and lives all about our need to *perform*.

Now let's be clear — feeling important and wanted and validated isn't bad. It's not wrong. But many of us have created a trap for ourselves where we believe this positive attention — on its own — is love.

Attention is merely the fast-food cousin of love. It may feel good at first, but without genuine, nourishing connection, it drags us down. Attention is dependent upon our ability to perform. Like a drug, it has us believe the only way we can feel better is to do more, achieve more, and prove more in order to earn more of it.

Love, on the other hand, is our inalienable birthright. Love builds us up, it strengthens us, it nourishes us. Love goes deep, while attention goes wide.

When we struggle with the discomfort and vulnerability that comes with love and genuine connection, we end up settling for the "drive thru" convenience of attention instead. And while seeking attention may seem satisfying in the short term, ultimately it's an exhausting way to address our innate need to love and to be loved. When we're able to build deeper, more genuine connections with ourselves and others, we'll find nourishment. We'll find that we are less dependent on "junk food" validation. We'll find that we don't have to strive so hard to accomplish as much in order to feel satiated, to experience the connection and peace of mind we truly want.

And so here's another gem I received through my work with Stutz that can help us break our addiction to constant validation. Instead of striving and manipulating and contorting and convincing ourselves that we need positive attention, we could simply let it go. As in, wake up every day and tell ourselves…

I let go of any hope that I'll be recognized or appreciated or elevated above others due to anything I do today.

Boom. Just take the self-image stuff right off the table. Go do what's important and quit worrying about anybody kissing our ass for it. Go do what will serve us and others, and give up any hope that we'll be appreciated for it. It's a bold, challenging practice, but ultimately it's an incredibly powerful and liberating stance to take.

So let's see. Let's put it into practice.

Think of an area where you're all butthurt because you're not getting the attention or appreciation or approval you want. Think of a place in your life where you believe you *need* others to praise you or give you some ovation. Maybe it's a spouse, a parent, or a child. Maybe it's a co-worker or a client. Or maybe, by god, it's just the whole world in general that doesn't get how splendid you are. Feel that friction? Great. Let's use it. Let's see what happens for you when you say to yourself…

I let go of any hope that I'll be recognized or appreciated or _____ due to anything I do today.

Change the wording to fit for your specific desires, and then notice what opens up. When I do this for myself or with clients, we notice an immediate sense of lightness. We loosen our attachment to what others say or do, and we feel our power return.

Many times, life becomes more simple when we free ourselves of the *need* for admiration or approval or recognition. This practice — and it is an *ongoing* practice, believe me — frees us up to be far more effective because we're not pissing away our energy jockeying for attention or recognition or adoration.

It short-circuits our belief that we have anything to prove, which means we get to take a look at our lives and ask, *If I'm no longer doing XYZ for recognition or approval, then why would I continue to do it? Why would I continue to tolerate this crap if it's not allowing greater freedom, aliveness, love, or peace?*

Now — if we get attention and recognition and adoration, then great. Soak it up. Enjoy it. But when we challenge our *need* for it, we may find that the freedom and aliveness and love and peace we ultimately want is much, much more accessible.

Practice this daily — if not hourly — and see if it opens your world and empowers you to play for what really matters.

Are You Willing to Be Hated and Misunderstood?

There's a saying where I come from: The further up the flagpole you get, the more people can see your ass. It points to the people-pleaser in each of us, one of our deepest commitments to do whatever it takes to avoid being criticized, hated, or misunderstood.

Over the years, as my work became more known in the world, I began to notice that I was increasingly fearful of how much of my ass was showing. Because there were more opportunities to be criticized and sniped, I was pumping the brakes. My work was becoming a drain because I was struggling to "get it right." I realized I was playing small.

So I brought this to Phil Stutz one day, and I was really hoping he had some mental tool that would magically vaporize the fear and send me on my way. I was hoping he'd deliver some painless, easy way to *avoid* this possibility of being wounded. Boy, was I wrong.

In his understated New York accent, he said to me, "So you want to avoid being hated and misunderstood?"

"Yeah, that sounds about right," I said.

"Okay. Then that's where we want to go. If we want to get stronger, then we want to go right into that fear."

Shiiiiiiiiiit. What have I gotten myself into this time?

I took a deep breath. Okay. Here we go. Bring it on.

No matter what we do in the world, people are going to like it or hate it. Because we're human, there are always going to be imperfections that others can use to take a shot at us. And as long as we're afraid of having someone misunderstand us or criticize us for what we've done, then we're going to strain everything we do through some filter. In order to try to please everyone, we're going to neuter whatever we have to contribute. Which means two things: (1) there's no way that we can stay completely safe from this stuff and (2) we betray and exhaust ourselves and give up our power trying to do so.

But on the other hand, imagine how much more powerful we would be if we were willing to embrace the possibility of being criticized and misunderstood. Imagine how much more powerful we would be if we stopped trying to avoid the inevitable and chose to do our work anyway.

Only the dead survive.

Look around. Find somebody that you admire, somebody that you truly appreciate for sharing their ideas and creativity in the world. Does everybody on the planet love and adore them? Or do they have critics and haters and snipers? Are they making excuses and hiding out? Or do they choose to create even though others may not like it?

Now, let's talk about what's possible for you. Grab something to write with and let's explore a new world. Answer these questions…

What do you currently do in your daily life to avoid being criticized or misunderstood?

How much time do you spend proving and explaining and justifying and defending what you say or think or want?

What would you do differently if you no longer had to defend or explain or justify what you wanted?

Now look at your answers. Is there anything in there that you could possibly experiment with today? Is there an opportunity to be bold and see if it's really true that getting some heat would be as bad as you imagined?

And how much more powerful would you be if you welcomed some kind of pushback because you knew it could make you stronger?

This is our opportunity to test what Bruce Lee said earlier. "Freedom discovers the man the moment he loses concern over what impression he is making or about to make."

Let's see.

And we can do so playfully. We don't have to make everything such a big deal. After all — comparatively speaking — we're basically a speck of dust on an infinitely small rock hurtling through one of trillions of galaxies in what is ultimately just a blink in a span of time our brains can't even begin to comprehend. Maybe — just maybe — whatever that mouth-breather Jerry has to say about your presentation isn't such a big deal.

Let's use that truth to put things in perspective. Let's use that truth to liberate us. Let's use that truth to play for what truly matters. Let's use that truth to play for something bigger than ourselves.

Meaning — Play for Something Bigger Than Yourself

One of the reasons most guys come to me for coaching is because they're sick of doing things the way they've been doing them. They're sick of their relationships and work feeling out of alignment. What used to light them up doesn't seem to do the trick anymore, and the thought of staying on this trajectory for another five months — much less five years — feels like a major drag.

They tell me things like, "It's no longer satisfying for me to just go out and make a buck. I want to do something that really matters. I want to do something that makes an impact." Personally, I went through this years ago, and it was one of the reasons why I sold my first company to become a professional coach. I absolutely *love* helping guys align their lives and professions with strength and meaning. So let's explore this idea of meaning so that we can understand how it relates to greater freedom, aliveness, love, and peace.

The I, We, All of Us Dartboard

Imagine a dartboard, and at the center of that dartboard — the bullseye — is you. Early on in life, especially in our teens and twenties, our circle of care is firmly at the center of this board. The story is all about us. *Who am I really? How can I make my mark in the world?* We're young, dumb, and full of, uh — whatever rhymes with "young" and "dumb" — and it's the time in our lives when we're breaking free from the influence of our parents and schoolmates to forge our own identity. And this will feed our fire — but only up to the point that it doesn't anymore.

So coming back to our dartboard, eventually our circle of care may expand a bit to include someone else. Someone special. We expand our circle of care from *I* to *We*. Now our efforts are more aligned with creating a life *with* someone else, maybe even some kids or aging family members. This can provide us with a rewarding sense of direction and meaning and satisfaction because we're serving the people we love and care about deeply. It can feed our fire up until the point that it doesn't anymore.

And this is the point where so many of us get stuck. We're repeating the same things that *used to* feed our fire — like seeing how much we can earn or being good providers for the people we care about — but we can't figure out what's missing.

Here's the thing — whether we realize it or not, our internal circle of care hasn't stopped expanding. If we go back to the dartboard we may find that, beyond just providing for ourselves (I) and the people we care about most (We), the circle has expanded to include All of Us — our tribe — the people who share our values, our worldview, and similar life experiences.

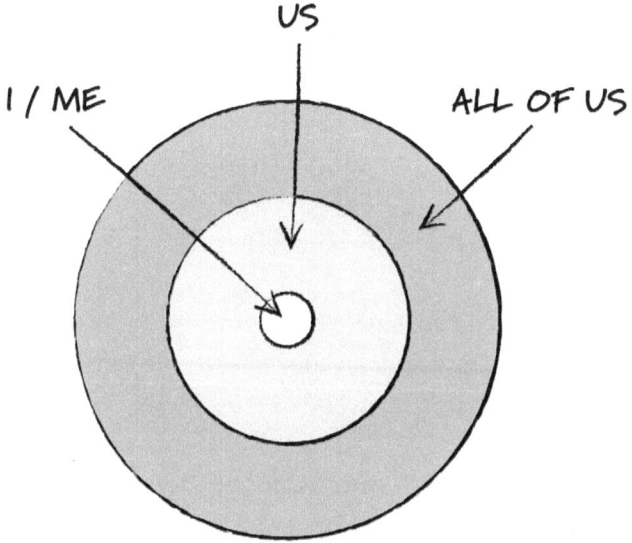

So when a guy comes to me, and he can't figure out why he's not feeling lit up anymore, often it's because he's still stuck playing a game of I or We. He's still seeing himself as a provider for himself and those closest to him. He hasn't recognized that the game has changed. He hasn't recognized that it's time to play for something bigger.

Playing for Something Bigger Than Yourself

Meaning is one of the core contributors to our joy and fulfillment. Beyond our desire to make a buck or look good or keep the kids fed, it's a calling to play for something bigger than ourselves. It can be religious or spiritual in nature. Or it can be something that simply builds fellowship and positively impacts the people we choose to call our community. And, you guessed it, our need to protect or please or prove can block this deep desire to get out of our own way and serve others.

Here are some of the excuses and some constructive ways to counter them.

Who am I to think I can help others? I'm not perfect. I don't have my shit together.
Just go help somebody.

I need to protect my status. I need to ensure that I look good. I need to be important.
No, you don't. Just go help somebody.

Will this be profitable? I use money as a way to justify doing things with my time. I need to make money doing this.
No, you don't. Just go help somebody.

But what about my family? I can't sacrifice my time with them.
You don't have to. Bring them along and benefit together. Just go help somebody.

We want to challenge any idea or expectation or condition that tries to block us from simply doing what builds our fire. If we're willing to be bold, if we're willing to be playful, and we're willing to get over ourselves, then we'll open ourselves up to the true fulfillment that comes from empowering others, too.

But what if you're struggling to figure out *where* to find meaning?

Where Do We Find Meaning?

I've talked to so many folks who tell me all about how they want to change the world. They have these grand visions of a movement they want to create. They talk about raising money and writing checks to foundations and building an infrastructure and all of that kind of stuff. And while that is certainly important, and even necessary for certain causes, many times this kind of stuff is rooted in what sounds flattering to our self-image.

That's because when we get in the trenches and start doing the experiments and start gathering the data, guess where we find the most meaning and most fulfillment? It's not in the boardroom of some foundation. It's not at the fancy dinner table of some fundraising event.

It's where we can look into someone's eyes and *see* that we're making a difference. More specifically, it's where we're directly impacting those who are going through a challenge that's very similar to one that we've gone through.

And that's because we tend to find the deepest enjoyment and fire by helping some version of ourselves from the past. It could be who we were twenty minutes, twenty months, or twenty years ago — most often our joy and fulfillment comes from seeing ourselves in others and helping them go through the challenges we've already overcome.

This could be teaching a kid to throw a ball, or helping an elderly woman find a light bulb in the hardware store. It could be personal troubles with substance abuse, professional challenges as a young entrepreneur trying to find funding, or spiritual dilemmas for someone who has lost their connection with what really matters. It doesn't matter how big or small the challenges may be.

Simply making it a daily practice to do one thing that's considerate for a stranger opens us up to great reward — especially if we let go of any expectations that we'll be celebrated in return. That's because when we get over ourselves, we spend less time grandstanding or hiding out. We learn from experience that the doorway to freedom, aliveness, love, and peace opens up when we get out of our own way.

This is how we bring out the best of who we are. This is how we transcend the limitations of our egos and defenses. This is how we transcend the never-ending conflicts and differences to see all that we have in common. And this is how we reconnect with all that we are — and all that simply is.

Conclusion

Back to the Butt Doctor

Perhaps you recall the introduction of this book — the story about the doctor, the nurse, and yours truly bent over a table, right? Sure you do. That introduction was written to help us understand expectations. And one of the expectations we may have about creating big changes in our lives is that it'll be dangerous. It'll require draining, herculean effort.

But that's not really true. As we've discussed throughout this book, when we're willing to find little opportunities to be bold, be playful, and get over ourselves, then the true dangers we face are often far smaller than we imagined. The *experiences* we truly want are much, much closer than our fears will allow us to believe. By engaging our challenges intelligently, we can find the sweet spot that has us feel more alive and expansive. We don't have to wait until we've crossed some fairy-tale finish line in order to experience greater peace of mind. We often find peace when we simply start aligning our actions out in the world with the values inside our mind and heart.

So let's take a minute to connect the dots and review the big takeaways from this book.

What Did We Learn?

First off, we learned that whether we know it or not, most of us are all living with a very clear purpose which is to avoid discomfort, risk (or loss), or humiliation. And even though we live in a cushy modern world, our primitive brains have adapted to believe that a threat to our discomfort, stability, or self-image is a threat to our lives. This helps us understand why there are so many of us are driving around in air-conditioned cars drinking $6 lattes and freaking out about how we're going to "survive."

Because we will always normalize and adapt to whatever level of comfort and safety and status we have, our brains will always find new threats. This perpetual escape, this pursuit of some magical finish line, is what puts us on the hamster wheel. It keeps us in a prey mentality, and we forget that we're actually hunters.

We learned that, beyond just feeling comfortable and safe and important, we want something more substantial for our lives. When we fantasize about *objective* achievements and outcomes and mountain summits and finish lines, we're really fantasizing about the *subjective* experience we hope they'll allow us to enjoy. And we know this because if we accomplished all of that stuff on our vision board and still felt trapped or drained or isolated or bored or stressed, then it would be a huge disappointment.

So this tells us that, whether we realize it or not, the *opposite* of those experiences is what we're playing for. Beyond comfort and security and acceptance, we ultimately want to experience some combination of freedom, aliveness, love, and peace. This understanding liberates us because it allows us to ditch the hamster wheel — the fantasy that *one day* we'll finally be set for life. It opens the door for us to find ways to allow these desired experiences into our lives today. No more waiting. No more excuses.

But this isn't some hedonistic "easy street" for life. When we prioritize freedom, aliveness, love, and peace, it means that we're going to steer directly into what *seems* dangerous. We're talking about discomfort, some financial risk, or looking like a weirdo from time to time. And so we learned how to recognize some of our most common excuses so that we could pivot into empowering action.

Given that our commitments to comfort, stability, and looking good are what keep us playing small, we then chose to take them on directly.

We learned that because avoiding discomfort eventually turns us into powerless, bitchy victims, it's essential for us to be bold — to own what we want and take responsibility for it. We learned how to use a pain in the ass as a doorway to clarifying what we want. And then we explored how we can choose to be an adult and own our power with maturity. We learned that discomfort is really just a *feeling*. We went through some basic, experiential practices so that we can increase our capacity for mental and physical discomfort — all in the service of greater strength.

Then we took on our second commitment — avoiding risk, loss, and missing out. When our brains dramatically overestimate the dangers we face, we end up severely limiting our options. Which means we typically only go for the "sure thing." And because so little in life is a "sure thing," this makes our existence extremely unsatisfying.

So we learned to challenge the monsters under the bed. *Is it really true we're in danger? Is it really true so much is at risk?* We learned that we have way more leverage when we understand that we don't have so much to lose. And we're much more effective when we're willing to say no to the shit that doesn't serve us anymore.

Instead of blindly bowing down to fear and pressure, we learned that we're much more powerful when we loosen up. We can be highly effective and find the fun by challenging the rules for how things have to be done. Instead of following the overburdened herd-of-hustle, we also learned that having a playful mindset helps forge our own unique path and do things on our own terms.

And then we took on the third commitment — to avoid humiliation or the possibility of looking like a moron. We put things into perspective, realizing that whatever *seems* like a big deal most likely *isn't* a big deal. We also learned how to use this as a reminder to not sweat the small stuff, to get out of our own way, and to play big when it comes to the experiences we most want in life.

We learned that when we're not defending our precious self-image, we're far more powerful and effective. We learned to ask ourselves, *What if there was nothing to prove?* Not to anyone alive or dead. Or even the voice inside our heads.

The same is true when we give up any hope of being admired or recognized or appreciated. We reclaim massive amounts of energy and focus when we drop the need to defend ourselves from being disliked or misunderstood.

This awareness helps us pull our heads out of our asses and focus on what we're doing and why we're really doing it. It opens us up to play for something much larger than our self-image. And it opens us up to greater meaning — our ability to positively impact others — which is essential to our peace of mind.

In a nutshell, we learned that life is a lot more fun and fulfilling when we're willing to be bold, be playful, and get over ourselves.

So one last thing before we wrap this up…

Brains, Balls, and Heart

I want this book to be a reminder to laugh at our fears and mistakes and shortcomings. It's a reminder that we don't need to be perfect. That even if we fall off the horse often, the key is to simply get back on.

It's a reminder to be kinder to ourselves. Because when we're kinder to ourselves, we're kinder to others as well. We tend to treat others the way we would want to be treated. And it's much easier to stay focused on what really matters when we're not having to clean up the messes that stem from being dicks to one another.

It's a reminder to tap into our curiosity, to reconnect with our essence — that part of us that is truly unique and in awe of this bizarre existence we call life. When we get lost in protecting and pleasing and proving, we eclipse our ability to recognize and experience the good, the true, and the beautiful that's all around us and within us. This book is a reminder to reconnect with the ineffable, inexplicable cosmic force that wants to be lived through us and as us. All of us.

I've been fortunate to see deep inside the lives of so many folks across different cultures and tax brackets. And the one thing that is always constant is love — our deep desire to be connected with one another. As we've discussed, our dreams of "success" are just theories for where and how we'll finally experience deep peace. And while the impact and accomplishments may be nice, we don't grieve for that stuff when a loved one passes away. We miss *that person*. We grieve losing our *connection* with them.

So this book is a reminder that, more than "succeeding," the most rewarding thing we can do is to love. And while choosing to love certainly isn't safe, if we're willing to be bold, playful, and get over ourselves, then expressing our genuine care and concern for others opens us up to the deep sense of freedom, aliveness, and peace that we most want *today*. Not later. Not once we've got XYZ handled. Not once we've earned this or proven that. If we're willing to challenge our fears, we can find opportunities to practice loving right now. We don't have to wait.

Because it's love that allows us to live with a deep appreciation for all that we already have.

It's love that allows us to forgive and accept ourselves and others simply as we are.

It's love that allows us to set firm, fierce boundaries against anything that makes us weak.

It's love that allows us to recognize and draw out the best in ourselves and one another.

It's love that allows us to *be* who we truly are.

And it's love that allows us to be one of the rare, extraordinary men on this planet who live with brains, balls, and a big, open heart.

So here's to a life of freedom, aliveness, love, and peace. Thank you for joining me on this ride. It doesn't last long, so let's play.

ACKNOWLEDGEMENTS

First, a big thank you to Ben Allen. Without your initiative, enthusiasm, and persistence this book wouldn't have been written. Writing this book has made me a better coach and leader, and I owe much of that to you.

Thank you to David Hooper. I feel so fortunate to pull from your expertise in book production, podcast production, and promotion. We've gone through the coaching process together, and your experiences have helped me make this book stronger as a result.

I'm grateful to Jodi Compton and Brooks Becker for reading (and correcting) every single word in this thing. Thanks to Rene Otero for the illustrations and graphics support. And thank you, David Provolo for lending your creative skills to the design and feel of the book.

I want to thank every single coaching client that I've had the chance to work with. Every story and every idea in this book had to filter through our conversations. I knew that if an idea or practice didn't help you move the needle in your life, then it didn't deserve to be in this book.

Gratitude to the hundreds of guests I've featured on The New Man Podcast. Being able to learn directly from so many extraordinary men and women is such a gift. Thank you for sharing your knowledge and wisdom with me and those that listen to the podcast.

Thank you to those who had my back throughout this process, those who were just an email or phone call away. I'm talking about Alex Gibson, Marc David, Ray Brejcha, Geoff Hanzlik, Craig Revord, Brian

Johnson, Eric Davis, Jeff Boss, Eric Goodman, Jaimal Yogis, Gerry Campbell, Britta Alexander, Keith Martin-Smith, Daniel Priestley, Mark Manson, and AJ Jacobs. Each of you responded when I asked for help, and that means a lot to a guy who has a hard time asking for help.

A big, big thank you to Phil Stutz for the direct help you've provided me in my life — and also for the major contributions you and Barry Michels have made to the themes of exoneration, resistance, and getting over yourself that are at the core of this book. Thank you to Chris Burris, LPC LMFT and Dr. Will Vanderveer for taking time out of your schedules to help me keep those clinical ducks in a row.

I want to thank the men and women I've had the opportunity to learn from and grow with in various men's groups, communities, and trainings over the years. From the jungles of Costa Rica to Tallahassee to Austin to Boulder to San Francisco to Los Angeles and many points in between, I've absorbed and learned so much from each of you. Simply being with you has made me a better man, husband, father, and coach.

I want to thank some of the coaches and teachers I've had along the way. Some of you I've had the opportunity to work with directly, and others I've gained so much from indirectly. This includes Ken Wilber, David Deida, Rich Litvin, Sean Dennison, Christiane Pelmas, Stephen Pressfield, Steve Chandler, Michael Neil, Abbot Jun Po Denis Kelly, Dennis Merzel (Genpo Roshi), Diane Musho Hamilton, Byron Katie, Don Miguel Ruiz, and S. N. Goenka.

To comedians like Eddie Murphy, Dave Chappelle, and Chris Rock — thank you for demonstrating how to be bold and playful. I consider you teachers as well. Thank you for reminding us not to take ourselves too seriously.

I'm aware that I'm unintentionally leaving out many others, so please know that this list of teachers, influences, and helpers is by no means complete.

To my dad — you've taught me how to be playful, to stick it out when I wanted to quit, and to "eat dessert first." I've always been so proud that you were my dad, and now that I'm also a father, I appreciate you so much more. To Nancy — I can't imagine life without you supporting me and Dad. From early on, you've always shown me love and support. I'm not sure if I can ever convey how much you mean to me. Thank you so much.

And, of course ...

To my wife, Alyson. You are my true ally. Throughout this writing process, you've endured hours upon hours of me rambling on about my ideas and doubts and fears and confusion. And through it all you believed in me the whole time. Having you by my side throughout this creative process was yet another lesson in what it means to be loved. Thank you for being my lover, my wife, my challenger, my support, and the mother of our amazing daughter. Thank you for encouraging me to be bold, to take risks, and to make sure I never take myself too seriously. And thank you for usually being the only person in the room who laughs at my tasteless, inappropriate jokes.

And to my daughter, Be. I want you to know that by simply being here on this planet, you have healed me and made me more complete. More than any other coach or teacher or guide, you have taught me how valuable this present moment can be. You've taught me that I'm capable of loving so much more than I ever thought I could. Being your father is such a gift, and I thought of you the entire time I wrote this book. I thought about the lessons I would want you to learn just in case I wasn't around to share them directly. I wrote this book in hopes that it would make the world just a little bit better for you and those you love.

And — I'll be honest — I also wrote this book in hopes that you'd be less likely to marry a douchebag.

ABOUT TRIPP LANIER

Tripp Lanier coaches men to get out of the rat race, become an authority in their field, and make a great living doing meaningful work they love. From small business owners, to startup founders, to Navy SEALs — Tripp has coached anyone and everyone who refuses to settle, play it safe, or follow the herd. As host of The New Man Podcast, he's racked up millions of downloads conducting interviews with extraordinary thinkers in business, personal growth, and spirituality. He lives a quiet, simple life with his wife and daughter near the beach in North Carolina.

Learn more at TrippLanier.com and TheNewManPodcast.com.

NEXT STEPS

Be sure to check out all of the free podcast, resources, and guides available at TheNewManPodcast.com.

And if you'd like to learn more about Tripp's coaching programs just visit TrippLanier.com.

www.ingramcontent.com/pod-product-compliance
Lightning Source LLC
Chambersburg PA
CBHW060524080526
44586CB00012B/608